Employment health and working environment in selected units of visakhapatnam Special Economic Zone

ANNAVARAPU LAVANYA

CONTENTS

Page No.

CHAPTER-I
INTRODUCTION

1.1 Origin of Special Economic Zones:

An 'Export Processing Zone' (EPZ) in simple terms can be defined as an industrial zone with special incentives, set up to attract foreign investors, in which imported material underwent some degree of processing before being exported again[1]. EPZ can be viewed as a clearly delineated industrial estate, which constitutes a free trade enclave in the customs and trade regime of the country, and where foreign manufacture firms producing mainly for export, benefit from certain factors and financial incentives[2]. However, the above given definitions are not concrete and there are many exceptions. Some Export Processing Zones may not be demarcated by physical boundaries as in cases where free trade applies throughout the countries, such as in the city states of Singapore and Hong Kong (previously), which are EPZs in themselves. Similarly China's 'Special Economic Zones' are on such a large scale that they seem to evade the above definition of EPZ[3]. The words 'SEZ' and 'EPZ' are used synonymously in this Study.

The concept of EPZ is known by different names such as Free Trade Zone, Industrial Free Zone, Maquiladoras (Mexico), Special Economic Zone (China). There are no less than 19 terms to describe what is, basically, the same concept. "Whatever be the terminology, the significance of the 'Export Processing Zones' lies essentially in its physical, social and economic separation from the rest of the country"[4].

1.2 EPZ: Past and Present:

There has been considerable growth in Export Processing Zones in size as well as in number over the last few decades, but the concept is not a new one. "Under the Roman Empire free trade zones were set up along the commercial routes, used for storing duty free goods before re-exporting them were a marginal element in a mercantile economy. The free towns of Middle Ages and the duty-free ports of the British Empire (Singapore, Gibraltar, and Hong Kong) continued the tradition"[5].

One of the International Labour Organisations (ILO) reports gives the earliest reference to such zones and it could be traced back to 13th century in Spain. According to the Report:

"*King Alfonso X granted certain commercial privileges to the city of Cadiz. The Free Zone Consortium of Cadiz was founded in 1929. Elsewhere in Spain, a free trade zone was set up in Barcelona before the First World War but due to civil war it did not really take off until after the Second World War when a number of automobile plants were established there*"[6].

The first export processing zone of modern era was set up in 1959 at Shannon, in Ireland. In 1962 the concept was adopted by Puerto Rico with the establishment of an EPZ in the Island. The concept soon spread to Asia. India was the first country to establish EPZ at Kandla, in the Asia Pacific Region in 1965. Sixteen years later there were nearly 175 EPZs spread across 50 countries. Since then export processing zones have been created in nearly half of the countries of the World mainly in the Third World. According to the ILO (1998) figures there are some 850 export processing zones world wide, employing almost 27 million people. The global distribution of zones by region, as per the figures provided by World Export Processing Zone Association (WEPZA) is given in the Chart below.

CHART- 1.1 DISTRIBUTION OF EPZs BY REGION : 1997

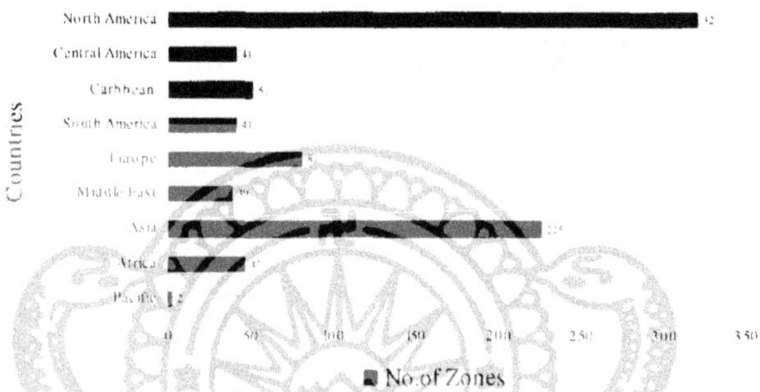

Source:World Export Processing Zone Association and International Labour Organisation.

CHART-1.2: NUMBER OF ZONES IN KEY COUNTRIES

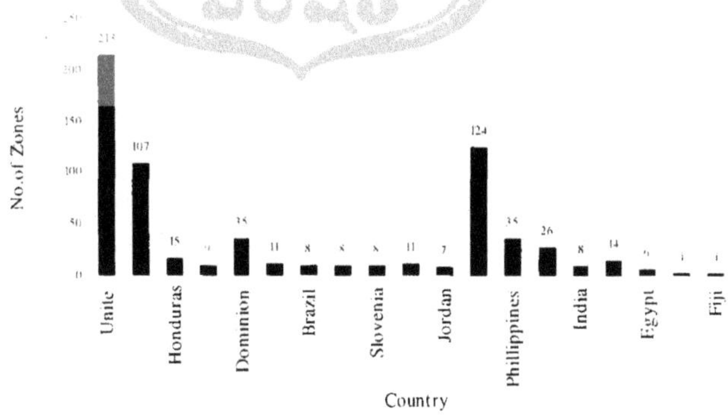

Some of the important countries with their respective number of zones are given in the Table below.

TABLE-1.1

Number of Zones in Key Countries.

Key Countries	No. of Zones
United States	213
Mexico	107
Honduras	15
Costa Rica	9
Dominican Republic	35
Columbia	11
Brazil	8
Bulgaria	8
Slovenia	8
Turkey	11
Jordan	7
China	124
Phillippines	35
Indonesia	26
India	7
Kenya	14
Egypt	6
Australia	1
Fiji	1

Source: World Export Processing Zone Association and International Labour Organisation

As evident from the Chart and the Table above, North America with 320 EPZs has the largest number of export processing zones followed by Asia which has 225 zones. Amongst the individual countries, United States with 213 zones has the largest number of EPZs, followed by China with 124 EPZs, and Mexico with 107 EPZs. Even though India was among one of the earliest countries to start a free trade zone, it has currently only 8 zones in the entire country.

In recent years the number of EPZs is increasing as more and more countries are authorising the development of private zones. The Philippines, for example is well known for its four government owned EPZs, but it has approved 83 zones, most of which are private[7]. In a similar manner Indian authorities have also approved the creation of at least three private EPZs[8].

1.3 EPZs in India:

The Government of India has announced its decision in the Lok Sabha in April 1960, to start Export Processing Zones in the Country. The first free trade zone was established at Kandla in 1965, which also happened to be the first in Asia, followed by SEEPZ (Mumbai), Falta (Calcutta), Noida (U.P), Madras, Cochin. Except SEEPZ all are multi-product zones where a variety of export products are manufactured and exported. SEEPZ is the Electronic Export Processing Zone at Santa Cruz, Mumbai. The Government has also permitted setting up of EPZs in private/joint sector. So far, only eight free trade and export processing zones (EPZs) are established in the Country. They are arranged in chronological order as follows:

1. Kandla Free Trade Zone (KFTZ), Gujarat (1965).
2. Santa Cruz Electronics Export Processing Zone (SEEPZ), Mumbai, (1975).
3. Falta Export Processing Zone (FEPZ), West Bengal, (1983).
4. Madras Export Processing Zone (MEPZ), Chennai, (1984).
5. Cochin Export Processing Zone, (CEPZ), Kerala. (1986).
6. Noida Export Processing Zone (NEPZ), Uttar Pradesh, (1994).
7. Visakhapatnam Export Processing Zone (VEPZ), Andhra Pradesh, (1994) and
8. Surat Export Processing Zone (SEPZ), Gujarat, (1994).

All these zones have been set up by Government of India with the support of respective State Governments and these are administered by Commerce Ministry. Each zone provides basic infrastructural facilities like tax holiday from corporate income tax for a period of five continuous years during the first eight years of production or operation.

1.4 Administrative Authority:

In India the EPZs are constituted as departmental undertakings under Ministry of Commerce, Government of India. Each zone is headed by a Development Commissioner, a civil servant, appointed by the Central Government. The highest decision and policy making body is the concerned EPZ authority, which is headed by the Minister of State for Commerce in the Central Government. It includes the Secretaries of all concerned Central and State Ministries as members as well as Development Commissioners of the EPZs in the country. The authority meets periodically to undertake a review of the EPZ and co-ordinates inter departmental issues. All approvals, licenses and other matters are dealt with by the concerned EPZ board, which meets regularly under the Chairmanship of the Additional Secretary, Ministry of Commerce. These Boards include representatives of concerned Ministries and act as 'single window clearance' for all issues pertaining to Zone operations. The States (in which the EPZs are located) have independent control over local taxes, municipal laws and incentives for different regions or types of industry in these EPZs.

1.5 The Special Economic Zones (SEZs):

A policy was introduced on 1.4.2000 for setting up of Special Economic Zones in the country with a view to provide an internationally competitive and hassle-free environment for exports. Units may be set up in SEZ for manufacture of goods and rendering of services. All the import/export operations of the SEZ units will be on self-certification basis. The units in the zone have to be net foreign exchange earners but they shall not be subjected to any pre-determined value addition or minimum export performance requirements. Sales in the Domestic Tariff Area by SEZ units shall be subject to payment of full Custom Duty and import policy in force. Further offshore banking units may be set up in the SEZs.

The policy provides for setting up SEZs in the public, private, joint sector or by State Governments. It was also envisaged that some of the existing Export Processing Zones would be converted into Special Economic Zones. In addition, approval has been given for setting up of 42 Special Economic Zones in various parts of the country in the private/ joint sectors or by the State Government.

1.5.1 Performance of the SEZs:

As on 31-3-2005, there are 811 units in operation in eight functional SEZs. Investments by the units in these zones are of the order of Rs.18309 million. The SEZ units provide employment to about 1,00, 650 persons out of which 32,185 are females. (31.98 per cent).

1.5.2 Export Performance of the SEZs:

Export performance of the SEZs in India for the year 2003-04 and 2004-05 are presented in Table – 2 and also depicted in Chart – 3.

TABLE-1.2

Exports from Special Economic Zones

Zone	2003-2004 (Rs.Crores)	2004-2005 (Rs.Crores)
Kandla – SEZ	1018.82	1060.14
SEEPZ –SEZ	7832.81	8298.59
Noida –SEZ	1534.17	4266.00
Madras –SEZ	1037.96	1376.91
Cochin –SEZ	298.91	462.99
Falta – SEZ	825.34	569.15
Visakhapatnam – SEZ	435.67	579.27
Surat – SEZ	869.90	1539.72
Total	13853.58	18152.77

Source: Ministry of Commerce and Industry, Department of Commerce, 2005.

CHART 1.3 EXPORT FROM SPECIAL ECONOMIC ZONES IN INDIA

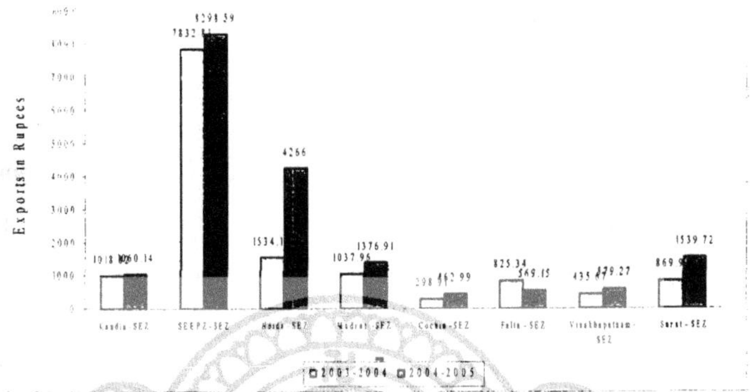

Source: Ministry of Commerce and Industry, Department of Commerce, 2005.

It may be observed from the Table 1.2 that except Falta – SEZ in all other SEZs value of exports in the year 2004-05 is higher than the previous year. However, the rate of increase in the value of exports differs. In the Visakhapatnam – SEZ the value of exports increased from Rs. 435.67 crores to Rs. 579.27 crores by 2004-05.

1.5.2.1 The Visakhapatnam Special Economic Zone:

The Visakhapatnam Export Processing Zone (VEPZ) is one of the governmental organisations established in the year 1989 in a total area of 366 acres with the aim of promoting export oriented goods and services. In the phase I, 163 acres of land was taken up for development and has been completed in the year 1995-96. The zone provides the necessary plot areas for factories of varying sizes with all the infrastructural facilities like power, water, internal roads, sewerage system etc. Visakhapatnam Export Processing Zone was converted in to

Special Economic Zone on First January 2003, by an ordinance issued by the Government of India on 1-4-2000.

1.5.2.2 Performance of the VSEZ:

At present 20 units are in operation in the zone such as computer system, aluminum alloy, leather garments, textiles garments, optical, recycled shop. polishing, food processing and diamond processing etc. most of these units are labour intensive thereby generating a lot of employment opportunities. The total employment provided by VSEZ at present is 2,692 of which 1,090 (40.49 per cent) are women. Imports and Exports of VSEZ units are presented in Table-3 and also depicted in Chart – 4.

TABLE-1.3

Imports and Exports of the VSEZ from 1997-98 to 2003-04

(Rs. in Crores)

Year	Imports	Exports
1997-98	0.49	0.04
1998-99	9.91	9.21
1999-2k	64.00	68.22
2001-01	148.80	149.97
2001-02	184.36	192.56
2002-03	259.95	361.89
2003-04	395.20	478.12
TOTAL	1062.71	1260.01

CHART-1.4 EXPORTS AND IMPORTS OF VSEZ FROM 1997-98 TO 2003-04.

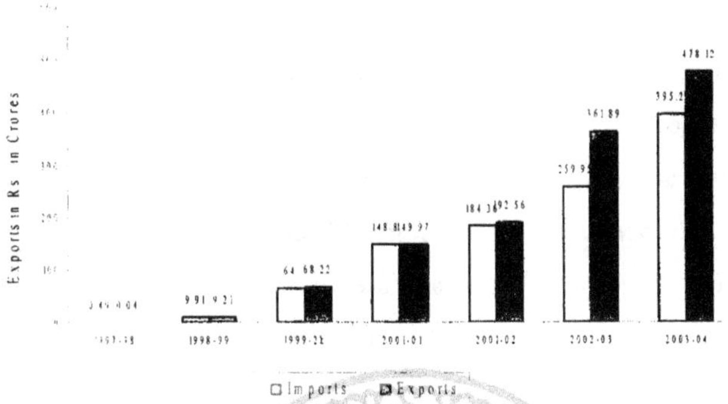

1.5.3 Women in the EPZs:

Women constitute a major proportion of workforce in EPZs but unfortunately their economic importance is not recognized at all. Even though women constitute the major portion (more than 35 per cent) of labour force in the EPZs, the jobs they do are always unskilled or low skilled. (Ashok Kundra, 2000)[9]. Employers are also reluctant to invest in developing the skills of women as they feel it as a waste of investment. However, the employees have a strong preference for women workers as it is believed that dexterity, patience and other specific attributes make them more suitable than men for carrying out tasks that demand painstaking attention to deal and are repetitive. Women regardless of their level of education constitute the bulk of unskilled and semi-skilled workforce and that is particularly pronounced in textiles, clothing, leather, electronics and diamond industries. EPZs have revealed strong preference for female workers in all the countries they operate. For example, in Bangladesh in Chittagong EPZ female workers account for 70 per cent and the remaining 30 per cent are males. The other problem in the zones is the exploitation of women in these zones. As per various studies,[10] the reasons for employing the women in the zone, particularly in electronics, garment and diamond industry, are certain inherent qualities possessed by women. These qualities, are either physiological, or a result of social conditioning like patience, concentration and willingness to undertake long hours of monotonous work. About 70 per cent of workers in EPZs are mostly from rural areas with poor economic background and are young and unmarried women with a little or no education. The turnover of this labour force is continuous to the EPZs. Employers prefer young and unmarried women who have least family responsibilities and therefore spend long hours with uninterrupted work (Ismail Hossain, 2001)[11]. There has been the other problem with regard to time schedule, particularly in assembly units. For example, in MEPZs it is observed that many units will not allow women to go to toilets while the work is pending. No special facilities are provided for women in the zones despite their presence in large numbers. Women are not given any maternity leave. Sexual harassment is one of the problems which is affecting a large number of women in the zones. From this, it may be concluded that several problems relating to the working conditions and environment of women workers in EPZ need the attention of appropriate authorities.

1.6 The Problem of the Study:

Export Processing Zones constitute an important element of promotion in developing countries. Besides developing physical infrastructure, they provide physical and taxation incentives to attract overseas investment. Boosting of exports, foreign exchange earnings, foreign investments, technology transfer, stimulating FDI, generating employment and developing forward and backward linkages have been the major objectives of EPZs.[12] The EPZs works to the advantage of the both the investors and the host country. The host country is able to earn foreign exchange and generate employment and the foreign investors gain the competitive edge by drafting cheap labour and other inputs in the process of manufacture.

The concept[13] is based on the rationale of Ricardian theory of comparative advantage. Developing countries beset with capital scarcity, lack of technical, managerial and institutional marketing skills are unable to step-up exports over a short period of time. Moreover, the institutional and physical infrastructure facilities are inherently poor. EPZs make up these deficiencies to some extent in a limited area to attract foreign investment. These measures help investors to capitalize on the low labour, rental and raw material costs.

Most of these units are labour intensive. Employment generation is an important objective of EPZs / SEZs and they help, in generating additional employment, but their overall impact depends upon the size of the economy and stage of its development. In smaller economies, successful EPZs have a significant proportion of workforce in the manufacturing sectors. This is true of EPZs in Mauritius, Mexico and Dominican Republic[14]. In Singapore, Malaysia and Sri Lanka, EPZ employment constitutes a higher proportion of overall industrial employment, which ranges between 16 to 35 per cent. In Hong Kong, Mexico, Korea and Taiwan it is estimated to be between five to six per cent. EPZ employment is not substantial in India as their number is small and the size is modest. However, Chinese Export Processing zones have generated considerable employment in view of their large size and broader scope of permitted activity.

Apart from direct employment, EPZs also create opportunities for indirect employment through backward linkage with local supplies of components and raw materials and in the service and construction sectors. The feature of the structure of employment in Export Processing zone relating to sex, age, marital status, educational background and previous work experience of the worker determines productivity and wage levels. According to the Ministry of Commerce, Government of India, at present there are 681 units in operation at eight functional Special Economic Zones spread over the country. The total employment in these zones is 94, 968 out of which 61, 231 are males (64.48 per cent) and 33, 737 are females (35.52 per cent). They are broadly distributed under the product group of electronics, light engineering items, chemicals and allied product, gem and jewellery, textiles, garments, plastics and rubber products.

1.7 Need and Significance of the Study:

A unique feature of EPZ employment structure is its feminisation due to the over whelming presence of electronics, gem and jewellery, textile and garment units. Assembling operations in these units are repetitive in nature and require low-level skills for which women are popularly considered to be more eminently suited. It has been observed that employment of women workers is high in the garment, gem and jewellery industry, next only to data processing and electronic assembling units. Employers have a strong preference for women workers since it is believed that dexterity, patience and other specific attributes make them more suitable than men for carrying out tasks that need painstaking attention to detail or repetitive. Women regardless of their level of education constitute the bulk of the unskilled and semi-skilled workers and that is particularly pronounced in the textile, clothing, leather, knitwear, electronics, optical and diamond industries (Kundra, 2000)[15].

"Skill development programme involves learning by doing," workers are drawn mainly from the rural unskilled female category that learned their skills through work under a supervisor for a period of time. If, after the specific period, she cannot graduate to the permanent category she will again undergo supervised training for another term. Skill development through learning by doing continues at other stages of operation as well (Gupta, 1996)[16].

Though the EPZs are achieving their objective of promoting exports they failed in achieving the objective of improving the welfare or working environment of weaker sections especially the women. Therefore, they need to examine the employment conditions of women workers and how the women were exploited in the units established in EPZs in general and VSEZ in particular. To make appropriate policy intervention this study is an attempt in that direction.

This present Study of women workers in VSEZ is a modest attempt to understand the problem of women in the area of employment, wages, working hours, working conditions, welfare facilities, trade unions, working environment and health hazards.

The Visakhapatnam Export and Processing Zone (VEPZ) is one of the governmental organisations established in the year 1989 in an area of 366 acres with an aim of promoting export oriented goods and services. During the first phase of development 163 acres of land was taken up and has been completed in the year 1995-96. The zone had processed the necessary plot areas for factories of varying sizes with all the infrastructural facilities like power, water, internal roads, sewage system etc. At present 20 units are in operation in the zone such as computer system, aluminum alloy, leather, leather garments, textiles garments. optical. recycled shop. polishing. food processing and diamond processing etc. Most of these units are labour intensive there by generating lot of employment opportunities to a considerable size. The total employment provided by VSEZ at present is 2692 of which 1602 are males (59.51 per cent) and 1090 (40.49 per cent) are women. The total employment increased from 10 workers in 1996-97 to 2692 workers in 2004-05. The VSEZ is thus providing employment to women at the rate of about 40 per cent of its employees. The women workers have increased from 100 in 1997-98 to 1090 in 2004-05. Though 20 units are in operation, the female employment is mainly concentrated in four units. These units are World Wide Diamond Industry, L.I.D. Jewellery, Madras Knitwear and Bangalore swatter industries. About 40 per cent of women workforce indicates that the employers of the units of VSEZ have a strong preference for women workers, as they believe that the women had dexterity, patience and other specific attributes more suitable for carrying out tasks of their establishments, generally of painstaking and repetitive nature. Therefore, the women regardless of their education and skill are found in VSEZ particularly in textile, clothing, leather, electronics and diamond establishments.

Though there are several studies on EPZs in general, the studies pertaining to women employees and their problems in the organisation are very few. Much of the studies are confined to EPZs exports and imports, investment, management and general working conditions etc.

These are a few reasons for the Study of the employment and working environment of women workers in VSEZ.

Introduction of female labour started in early 1980s. This is because of modern technology, non-militant nature, steady and sincere workforce, female non-desire to entrepreneur. Employment opportunities have increased for females in these units, which have gone up by 20 per cent within a span of 50 years of time. Though there is no strict decision of labour on the basis of gender, females are mostly employed in the EPZs particularly in diamond, knitwear, leather, swatters, gems and jewellery due to their trustworthiness, sincerity and steadiness. The other reasons like increase in import and export activities have also contributed to the steady increase of women workforce.

Gem and jewellery units, which are employing female labour force, are in unequal number to male workers. Female labour is not used in modern process but in traditional, repetitive process where skill is not of much value. However, opportunities for female labourforce have been increased but it has lead to exploitation of female labour. The women employees in EPZs particularly in diamond and knitwear industries suffer from problems ranging from insecurity of employment, lack of standard minimum wages, excessive hours of work and absence of welfare amenities and various other forms of exploitation.

Though there are laws to enforce regular payment and prevention of unfair deduction of wages, provision of regular working hours, laws and holidays, proper environment, supply of drinking water and social security against old age, sickness in human working conditions, low trade unions etc. there is no effective government machinery to monitor the implementation of these laws in the interest of workers in general and women in particular in these units in the VSEZ. K.Rama Prabha[17] study has shown 100 types of harassments in VSEZ. The study has identified that there are no festival holidays, no over-time wages, no maternity leave. Some studies like All India Democratic Women's Association[18] stated that the women workers are subjected to severe harassment by the employers who are not allowing the workers even the basic human and social life. The Christian workers who availed leave on Christmas day were suspended from 1 to 7 days; two workers who took the 'Ayyappa Deeksha' were suspended for one day. In one case, a woman was terminated immediately after her pregnancy was known, illegal deduction from salary, reasons for deductions like active in union, for not drinking tea, moving the stool, for casting vote in local body elections etc. Unable to bear the harassment and to improve the working environment, the workers of the unit under the Israeli management went on a strike from 9th January 2002.

The importance and significance of the present study thus, lies in unfolding and unraveling the various facts and figures in a systematic way pertaining to the problems of women employees and working environment of the women in these units in VSEZ in respect of the points mentioned above. The study is also focused at suggesting the remedial measures to improve the working conditions of women workers in VSEZ in general and the selected four units in particular.

1.8 Objectives of the Study:

The objectives of the study are:

a. To examine the socio-economic conditions of women workers in the four selected units in VSEZ;

b. To study the employment and working environment of women workers in these industries.

c. To assess the health problem of women workers in these industries.

d. To study the various forms of social, physical and economic exploitation which the women are subjected to, if any.

e. To suggest remedial measures for improving, social, economic and working conditions of women workers in these industries.

1.9 Data Base and Methodology:

The present Study is based on a sample survey of four units operating in Visakhapatnam Special Economic Zone in Visakhapatnam, covering a sample of 311 workers employed in these plants. The four units are World Wide Diamond (WWD), Madras Knitwear Pvt.Ltd. (MKW), Bangalore Swatters Pvt. Ltd. (BSW) and L.I.D. Jewellery Pvt.Ltd (LID). The survey was conducted during the period, January-June, 2004. The random sample of 311 women was from these plants, which gave permission to collect information from their workers. After getting the initial information about the plants and the workers, a structured interview schedule consisting of both close-ended and open-ended questions relating to socio-economic conditions, employment, working environment and health conditions of women workers was convassed. The collected data was coded and tabulated systematically. Finally, the data were analyzed by using descriptive measures of statistics, such as arithmetic mean, standard deviation, and percentage method. To test for the significant differences for certain characteristics linear multiple regression technique was employed wherever necessary and conclusions were drawn accordingly.

1.9.1 Methodological Problems:

Getting permission from the managements was the most difficult phase of data collection. Lot of strain was felt during the process. The list of plants was taken from administrative authority and the selection of units was taken randomly. During the first visit they suspected and enquired whether the researcher is from labour department. On clarification that the work is purely academic, then only some of them allowed the researcher to conduct interviews, but insisted to do it in front of them. In these units, permission is sought from the respective administrative offices of the units, situated in the zone premises. Two units created problems in giving permission by saying that the work is heavy and the employees could not be spared. Only after repeated requests and frequent telephone calls, they allowed the researcher to conduct the interviews. Though permission was given to interview the workers, statutory records were not shown to the researcher.

1.10 Plan of the Study:

The Study is organised in seven Chapters. Introductory Chapter deals with the problem stated against the backdrop of history of SEZs, role and significance of Indian SEZs. It also contains the objectives of the Study, database, methodology and methodological problems. A review of literature is presented in the second Chapter. The third Chapter is devoted to the presentation of the socio-economic profile of the women workers in VSEZ. The fourth Chapter presents the employment, health and working environment of women workers in VSEZ units. The fifth Chapter contains determinants of income of women workers in VSEZ units. The sixth Chapter analyses the problem of migration of women workers in VSEZ units. The last Chapter presents a summary of conclusions and policy implications of the Study.

References:

[1] ILO (1998): *Labour and Social Issues relating to Export Processing Zones*, p.3.

[2] Raman, R and Anant (1989): "A Review of Free Trade Zones in Developing Countries": *Indian Institute of Foreign Trade*. New Delhi. p.1.

[3] ICFTU (1998): "Behind the wire: Anti union repression in the EPZs", this information is present on the website of *ICFTU* under the heading EPZs.

[4] Raman (1989): *Op.cit.*

[5] ICFTU (1998): *Op.Cit.*

[6] ILO (1998): *Op.cit*, p.3

[7] Ibid, p.3.

[8]Government of India (1997-98): *Annual Report 1997-98*, Ministry of Commerce, New Delhi.

[9] Ashok Kundra (2000): *The Performance of India's Export Zone*, Sage Publications, New Delhi, p.79

[10] Kumar Rajiv (1982): *India's export processing zones*, Oxford University Press, India.

[11] Ismail Hossain (2001): *Export Processing Zones in Bangladesh and industrial relations*, Ed. by A.S. Oberoi & Others.

[12] Ashok Kundra (2000): Op.Cit.

[13] R.Thamargoshi (2001): *Promotion of social dialogue in EPZs in South Asia*, Synthesis of Experience. Ed. by A.S. Oberoi & Others.

[14] Indrani Mazumdar (2001): *EPZs and their work in India: A study of the Noida export processing zone*, Ed. by A.S. Oberoi & Others.

[15] Ashok Kundra (2000): *Op.Cit*, p. 81.

[16] S.P.Gupta (ed) (1996): *China's Economic Reforms: The role of Special Economic Zones and Economic and technological development zones*, Allied Publishers Ltd., New Delhi.

[17] Rama Prabha (2003): *CITU, VSEZ: EPZs and globalization past experience and future challenges,* Intl. Workshop organized by Solidarity Centre, Washington at Bangkok, Thailand from Oct. 8-11, 2003.

[18] AIDWA (2003): Rama Devi K.: '*Praja Sakthi*' Visakhapatnam, July.

CHAPTER - II

CHAPTER - II
REVIEW OF LITERATURE

2.1 Introduction:

In this Chapter an attempt is made to review the studies about the employment, health and working conditions of women at international and national level. This Chapter is divided into two Sections. Section I gives a the reviews related to employment and health and Section II gives a brief picture of the New Economic Policy on women in export processing zones.

The socio-economic advancement of a country can be best judged by the status and position it bestows on its women. The Constitution of India recognised equal status for women in independent India. particularly Article 16 guarantees equality of opportunity in public employment. Unfortunately, the status of women in the society did not become equal in all spheres of life. Prior to 1975, there were very few studies on women in India. Padmini Sengupta has written well before the international women's year on Indian women, highlighting the economic, political and social background of changes in the status of women in the post-Independent period.

As Pandit Nehru remarked, "*The greatest revolution in a country is the one that affects the status and living conditions of its women*". Today, because of the national need, the changing pattern of society and the desire to contribute towards the general good, and their own satisfaction and economic relief, women are emerging in various fields of services. Because of their increasing numbers as workers outside the home. world organisations, such as the International Labour Organisation, National Government and competent authorities are concentrating themselves more and more on the special problems, which married women with family responsibilities face and in giving them equal opportunities. The consensus of opinion now is that it is almost inevitable that women will work, no matter what the motivation is, and they should be helped by the society as a whole so that the hitherto dormant women power can be harnessed to make women an integrated part of a stable working force[1].

The changing world has brought many new interests into women's orbit and altered the pattern of domestic life. India is a developing country and as such its women do not take enough active part in the economic reconstruction of their motherland. The Ministry of Labour and Employment, Government of India[2] has pointed out that four factors prevail in bringing women to work. They are inadequate income of the principal earner, temporary mishaps, death of the breadwinner and a woman's desire for economic independence for securing higher standard of living. With the Independence of India, the position of women has been further raised by the enactment of various sections of the Hindu code. The legal condemnation of the dowry system has also raised the status of women.

However, community policies and public opinion has to be created to help women to meet their multiple duties. Regarding re-entry into employment after childbirth, the employment policy convention 1964 and ILO advocate that women be a part of the integrated labour force on equal footing with men. In 1951 a convention concerning equal remuneration for men and women workers of equal value was adopted by the ILO and was ratified by India. The Planning Commission for the third plan period stated that "there will be need for a large number of women workers in various spheres of activity''.

SECTION – I

In this Section, an attempt is made to review International and National Studies regarding employment and health.

2.2.1 International Studies:

The Statutory Commission declared that the women movement in India may achieve great results. Even though the position of women before independence was not well defined, there were laws regulating the conditions of employment and work of women during their life cycle and support services to be provided for working women. Women engaged in large and small trades have increased rapidly. No country created a more outstanding records in the state employment of women than India when she appointed a woman Ambassador, Governor, and Minister in the Centre. Neither were these high-level officials mere solitary instances of brilliant women. They were and are backed by their own sex in almost every sphere of national activity. One sees women in every office now, working equally with men. A number of careers are now open to women[3].

There are two approaches to women's participation in economic activity. According to the first, labour force participation is residual to women's responsibility for childcare and other domestic work. The alternative approach is that women participate in wage labour regardless of childcare or domestic work since there is economic pressure, which is overriding the domestic responsibility. These two approaches reflect the neoclassical view that work outside the home is conditioned by household choices between income and leisure and appear to consider women's domestic responsibilities as alternative to wage work. Non-participation in labour market does not entitle women to leisure. Domestic work is not a leisure time activity. Despite cultural, regional and temporal differences, women combine domestic work with wage work and the discrimination of the former has not been substantial because of the latter.

Sunder[4] points out that the advanced and labour-scarce economies present a different picture of women labour. Skilled and highly qualified manpower has become a scarce resource. Economic development, modernisation and growth do not necessarily ensure that their benefits reach the poorest and the weakest. It is further observed that polices to reduce unemployment and promote expansion of employment opportunities do not lead to an improvement in female employment. Women workers in India constitute 33 per cent of the total workforce and their share in unemployment is 40 per cent which is evidently higher than their share of total work force. However, women employment is not given proper focus and it is not considered as a specific category.

In the developed industrial countries of the West labour force constitutes 48.5 per cent of the population and the percentage of women in labour force is also equally high at 40 per cent. Throughout developed countries women workers earn on an average between 50 per cent and 85 per cent as those of the males. In advanced countries more and more women go out to work. But the emphasis is on 'going out' rather than on work[5]. Women workers in US formed 15 per cent of the labour force in 1870 and this has increased to 36 per cent in 1970 and 53 per cent in 1986. Women labour force in Japan is 49 per cent of the total labour force[6]. It tops the list in women workers being 610 for 1000 males.

Similar figures were also seen in Sweden at 66 per cent, UK 38.7 per cent, Israel 33.6 per cent and USA 41.5 per cent. It is to be noted that in US, UK, Canada, Japan and Sweden married women are nearly 60 per cent of the women labour force[7].

The women labour force trends have interesting insights in various countries of the world. In the US the total labour force has increased from 41.6 millions in 1920 to 82 millions in 1970 and the number of women in the labour force increased from 8.5 millions to 31.0 millions during the same period. Since 1960s, there has been an influx of a larger force which increased by 32 million workers between 1966 and 1998. Of this women have accounted for an increasing share of the labour force and this trend is projected to continue at least through the early 1990s. However, economists attribute this to the significant decline on productivity and growth. Between 1966 and 1980 the average annual productivity decreased from 3.37 per cent per annum to 0.93 per cent per annum[8].

ILO[9] uses two estimates to assess women work force participation on a global level. They are crude activity rates (for all ages) and refined activity rates (for 15-64 years). The ILO has projected that over 1000 million female or nearly one third of the world's female population will be economically active in the year 2000 A.D. There is a greater under-estimation of female work force in developing countries than in developed industrialised countries.

2.2.2 National Studies:

Employment trend since 1971 is essential to draw inferences as to current employment status of women and for future policy making. The size of employed women has certainly swelled in the past two census periods. According to the 1991 census, the female population was 264 million, out of which 132 million females were in the working age group of 14-50 years. Though legal and Constitutional protection has been conferred on women, social attitude is still obstructionist, and it is hard to break the notion that feminine and professional role expectations are mutually exclusive[10].

Ghosh[11] observes that according to the Census of India the workforce participation rate for the female was found to have dropped from 28 per cent in 1961 to 14.2 per cent in 1971 but rose to 21 per cent in 1981. According to the 58th round (July- December 2004) Survey of NSSO, the female work force participation rate in rural areas declined to 281 per thousand compared to 299 in the 55th Round (July 1999-2000). In urban areas it increased marginally from 139 to 140. In rural areas, 85 per cent of women workers are engaged primarily in agricultural activities and related sectors such as animal husbandry. In urban areas, a significant proportion of women workers are employed in the unorganised sectors such as household industry, pretty trade and services, and building and construction activity. According to a National Institute of Public Finance and Policy (NIPFP) study on Gender Budgeting the average female's wage is almost 80 per cent of the male average in urban areas, while it is less than 60 per cent of the corresponding male rate in rural areas. Employment of women in the organised sector (both public and private) as on March 31st, 2002 is 4.95

million, which constitutes 18.1 per cent of the total organised sector employment in the country, compared to 17.9 per cent in 2001. The distribution of women employees across industries reveals that community, social and personal services sectors employed 56.5 per cent of women workers followed by manufacturing (20.6 per cent), agriculture and allied occupations (9.4 per cent) and finance, insurance, real estate business (5.2 per cent). The proportion of women in organised sector employment is higher in States with higher female literacy rates. Improvement in the quality of women's employment depends upon increased access to education and skill development training. Several initiatives have been taken to provide training for women. There are about 776 institutes (224 Women Industrial Training Institutes and 552 Women Wing in General Industrial Training Institutes (ITI/ Private ITI) providing about 47,472 training seats for vocational training facilities for women at craft man level[12]. According to National Commission on self-employed women and women in the Informal Sector, (Sharma Shakti, 1988) around 94 per cent of the female workforce is concentrated in this sector. Due to diverse nature of operations, which do not come under the purview of Factories Act (1948), it is very difficult to estimate the extent of employment generation and total value added to products in this sector.

Many studies reveal that participation in economic activities does not necessarily enhance the social status of women. Regardless of the economic systems or the form of economic production, the social force and norms affect the status of women. Employment of women does not lead to economic independence or control over earnings. What exactly determines the male-female differences in the work field is yet to be ascertained and most studies have not helped in understanding the processes, and economic explanations are but partial[13].

Most studies conducted in India on the social and economic condition of labour of different classes, like urban and rural have been on male workers. This bias is due to the fact that female workers were overshadowed by the male workers both in terms of absolute numbers and rate of growth. Moreover most of the studies on women have focused on the status of women with detailed accounts on the position, activities and role of women in different tribes, castes and communities. By and large, the approach has been sociological with very marginal attention to the economic aspects of women.

The socio- psychological attitudes of educated working women was the theme of Kapur's[14] study, which concludes that employed wives make marital interaction a little more complicated and create adjustment problems in the family owing to their multiple roles coming in conflict with their expected and actual conduct.

On the basis of ILO data[15] it is observed that since World War II, the volume of female labour force has gone up and structurally there has been a shift in favour of service sector jobs, the same phenomenon is also noticed even among the developed countries. Alam[16] revealed that the role of Assam women in the household is very significant. Jagadish Prasad[17] observed that the female participation rate in the labour force in different regions of Bihar is remarkably low. He further observes that even this employment is very low-earning which demands strenuous and drudgery work in low skill and low technology sectors of low productivity. Godgil[18], Ashok Mitra[19], Sinha[20] and Ambannavar[21] studied the occupational distribution of women workforce in their pioneering and well-documented studies. Planning Commission[22] and National Commission on labour[23] demonstrated the growth of industries and occupations in which women usually have a substantial share in employment. The case study on women and urban development of Tirupati town[24] demonstrated the rapidly changing occupational pattern of women in recent years. Jayanti[25]reported that the role of women is significant in the development of Indian economy. Singh etal[26] pointed out that in a study of self-employed women in the resettlement colonies of Delhi, a very small proportion of women were considered primary earners. Manjudar[27] points out that the urban poor are the same as those in rural areas, both living at the bottom of the social structure and suffering from cumulative inequalities. Studies by Singh and De Souza[28] and Brahme[29] have shown how male absorption into the urbanising economy has helped the female employment in demanding jobs such as scavenging, swamping etc.

According to Sunder,[30] women's employment is divided into three categories. (1) Home-based activities which are either an extention of their household activities like dairying, poultry keeping, food processing, embroidery work, zeri work, lace making etc., (2) Home–based production using non-traditional and acquired skills like beedi rolling, machinery parts, retail trading, flower and vegetables vending, old garment selling, laundry etc. Boserup[31], brings out the women's role in economic development. She explains the role of sex in farming. The status of women in the family and the status of women in the labour market are two different things. The women status in the family may improve while her status in the labour market may deteriorate. This is likely to happen to middle class women at this stage when they are offered low grade office jobs or work while high status job or work continues to be a male prerogative. Bose[32] concluded that though the female labour force participation is influenced by the factor, but that is not the sole governing factor of female employment outside home. Radha Devi[33] concluded that the burden of household duties may not always contribute to withdrawal from work participation of women. She also analysed trends in women's employment in white collar occupation like, trading, mining, clerical etc., with the advent of industrialisation and modernisation, the traditional subsistence economy has been disturbed. The changing structure of employment, owing to the introduction of new crops for international market, changing land ownership and land tenure system leading to rural landlessness, technological innovations leading to displacement of artisans, had some impact on few women workforce in the informal sector of rural and urban economies. The changing structure of employment necessitated a shift in the skill requirement, which quizzed women out of independent productive activities and directed to market and forced them to work as domestic and casual workers.

In the third world countries the new international division of labour process has age-specific female labourforce. These young women are classified as semi-skilled or unskilled, based on the time requirement on job training. In the developed countries women cluster in the service sector. This includes teaching, nursing, childcare and food servicing. In developing countries although women in servicing sector form only a smaller proportion of the total female labourforce, their concentration is high in white-collar jobs. Women in the industry, both in developed and developing countries were clustered in factories producing textiles, garments, footwear, toys and goods etc.[34]

Employment pattern of women[35] in different regions in India show that women are employed in public as well as private sectors in various institutions. In the northern region rising trend of women employment is found in both public and private sectors during a period of one year. Similar trend is observed in central region and northern region in both sectors. In eastern region, changes of employment of women are found to be negative. In western region, women got employment opportunities in both public sector and private sector. In southern region, the employment opportunities in private sector decreased. Industry-wise distribution of women employment has shown that women were engaged in different industries such as agriculture, housing, mining and quarrying, manufacturing, electricity, gas and water, construction, wholesale and retail trade, transport and storage, financing and insurance, social and personal services.

Mahajan[36] says that the economic status of women is now accepted as an indication of an economy's level of development. Modernisation and economic development opened new areas to women. Social changes and education levels enabled women to enter new occupations, which are totally closed to them earlier. Ashok Mitra[37] observed that employment of women in organised sector has to be promoted so that the role of women will be enhanced in the over all development. This amounts to giving more weightage in the struggle to eliminate poverty and inequality. He also states that employment not only holds key to productivity but also to improvements in status of women. Usha Kundra[38] concluded that human resource is the most valuable asset of any country. Lalitha Devi [39] observed that employment of all types contributed in several ways to create women's power in society and this was reflected in many fields where customs and traditions had prescribed a subordinate role for women.

Sushma Singhal[40] concluded that in the current developing society and when inflation rate is so high, there is a need for the requisition of material goods so as to present a better level of living among their colleagues and acquaintances. This tendency is more common in urban areas than rural. This obviously puts greater pressure on females. This is one of the chief reasons today why women take up jobs outside their homes for family management reasons as well as to perform their traditional household duties. The changing social and economic conditions have compelled the women to actively participate in work and thereby earn extra income for the family.

In addition to IRD programme in 1982[41] for supplementing the assistance to women. Development of Women and Children in Rural Areas Scheme was started as a part of IRD programme in selected districts of different states. The objective of the scheme is to "focus attention on women members of the families of the target group so as to increase their income and also to provide needed supporting services to enable them to take income generating activities".

Many technological innovations further exacerbate class and gender inequalities. Women have a limited experience of modern agricultural production and very little experience of modern consumption. The Sixth Five-year plan contains a chapter on women and development. It also spells out the strategy to raise the status of women in the society, which include exploration of new avenues for income generating schemes. This major programme of poverty alleviation provided special efforts to ensure that the benefits in the form of loans and subsidies are directed towards women members of the households and at least 30 per cent of total families assisted during a year should be women beneficiaries.

According to one ILO Report (1985), out of 1800 million workers in the world, 600 million are women, constituting one third of global workforce. In India, a comparison of the Census data indicates that there has been an increase among female workers in rural areas. The work participation rate for female was higher in rural areas than in the urban areas. The development of rural women in India was firstl introduced in 1952. It made a modest beginning when the rural women were encouraged to form women's clubs, which came to be known as Mahila Mandals in most of the States[42].

The basic concept of a Mahila Mandal was to create opportunities for the rural women to improve their status through plans, policies and programmes with a view to generate employment in the rural areas and to enable women to enjoy the fruits of development. The government launched a series of programmes since 1987 such as Integrated Rural Development Programme (IRDP), Development of Women and Children in Rural Areas (DWCRA), Jawahar Rozgar Yojana (JRY) and Employment Assurance Scheme (EAS). Women constitute a major segment of rural society. They are often not able to reap the benefits of the government programmes due to various socio-economic reasons[43].

Employment is a must for the rural women to make them economically independent. It will enable them to stand on their feet. Being economically independent is a great boon to their self-confidence.

The society is bound to recognize their inherent qualities, their worth and their inalienable fights. Then only they will start getting respect from their family members as well. So, it is necessary to increase awareness among the women regarding available opportunities, their rights and responsibilities through education from grass-roots level in rural areas[44].

According to Yadav[45], traditional involvement of women in the retail fish trade has made them indispensable in this sector. The retail fish trade involves aspects of fish handling, preservation, processing, marketing, pricing, credit, borrowing, accounting, saving, etc. Women have shown their capabilities and adaptabilities to all aspects of skilled professions. In the process, their knowledge and interest is being passed on from generation to generation in a natural manner. Rural women in Orissa. West Bengal, Kerala, Bihar and some other parts of the country are expanding their activities to non-traditional livelihood and are undertaking new opportunities such as net weaving and mending, fish breeding, and commercial aquaculture.

The fact that Indian marine products are accepted world-wide and those exports have grown up to about Rs. 4,600 crores speak of the good job done by the thousands of women processing workers. Fish farming has gained roots in all parts of the country and is presently being considered as a viable means of employment for the rural population and women are expected to play a pivotal role on the furtherance of aquaculture.

Neeta Anand[46] examines how women contribute greatly to the economy. They are pioneers in various professions. Women are working in different sectors of the economy as agricultural labourers, road construction workers, domestic helpers, petty crafts women, self-employed women, doctors, engineers, lecturers, and white collared executives. Employment of women is an index of the states in society. According to Census data the work participation rate of women steadily raised from 14.22 per cent in 1971 to 19.67 per cent in 1981. The rise in work participation of women has been even steeper from 37.81 lakhs in 1991 to 47.74 lakhs in 1998. The UN statistics on women indicate that a majority of the female work force is involved in unpaid family work. Globalisation, urbanisation and privatisation have adverse effect on women employment. They are loosing employment due to technological changes, substitution of women labour and deskilling of women work.

According to 2001 Census methodology, which is more sensitive to measurement of unpaid women productive work, most female workers are involved in agriculture. They are agricultural labourers rather than cultivators. Apart from agriculture, women in rural areas are engaged in animal husbandry, weaving, handicrafts, tailoring, foresting, fish vending, sericulture etc. According to the latest round of NSSO in the year 1999-2000, there were nearly 393 million workers in the country, of which women workers numbered 122 million (constituting less than one-third of the total workers): 103 million in rural areas and 19 million in urban areas. The NSSO gives three estimates of employment or unemployment depending on the reference period used. The total number of women workers remained almost the same since the last Round in 1993-94, as population has increased during the period there was a decline in the workers participation rates for women in rural and urban areas[47].

The occupational break-up of the female work force reflects a gendered work structure. In the category of professional, technical and related work, women dominate in nursing and teaching. In the service sector which employs a large proportion of women, it is in the category of personal services that women dominate (housekeepers, maids, launderers, beauticians etc.). A large proportion of women workers are production process workers, largely in agriculture and related activities, which are located at the bottom of the labour hierarchy[48].

Even in women friendly sectors like banking and information technology, the latter allegedly having the potential to open up new avenues for women as a gender-neutral employer, such an outcome is not automatic. Women still account only for about 13 per cent of the total workers in banking. A recent study on the IT sector shows that while a large number of women are employed in this industry, most of them are at the lower end of the technology segment[49].

According to Duraiswamy (1997)[50] to a considerable extent gender disparity in employment and earnings arises due to societal attitudes towards women's education deriving from their perceived role of a homemaker, which constraints their access to higher education and training. However, it is also true that even among the high and equally educated women in the science and technology fields, there is gender discrimination in earnings for similar jobs. A case study for the states of Kerala and Tamil Nadu shows, the gender gap in earning of highly qualified persons, measured by the ratio of female to male earning is 0.78 in Kerala in the science and technology field. About 18 per cent of the difference can be explained in terms of the occupational segregation, 50-60 per cent by productivity characteristics, which suggests that almost a quarter is in terms of discrimination while changing family norms appear to favour working women, their choices in terms of nature and sector of work are restricted as also their aspirations for a career. While employment for women has increased in previously male dominated arenas with the growing flexibility in the work force, newer job opportunities are being created in a gender differentiated way.

There are two approaches to women's participation in economic activity. According to the first, labour force participation is residual to women's responsibility for childcare and other domestic work. The alternative approach is that women participate in wage labour regardless of childcare or domestic work since there is economic pressure which overrides the domestic responsibility. These two approaches reflect the neoclassical view that work outside home is conditioned by household choices between income and leisure. and appear to consider women's domestic responsibilities as alternative to wage work. Non-participation in labour market does not entitle women to leisure. Domestic work is not a leisure time activity. Despite cultural, regional and temporal differences, women combine domestic work with wage work and the discrimination of the former has not been substantial because of the latter.

Singh, Bhatty and Patel state that three-fourths of working women were unable to devote proper attention to their children as they have to spend most part of their time outside home. The role conflict is thus, closely related to the purpose of employment whether it is for fulfillment arising from educational achievement or economic independence. Chakravarthy's study on women farm-labour also points to the concepts of male superiority and tradition bound subservience of women, which remain quite undisturbed in spite of women's economic participation.

Most Indian studies reveal that women show work preference mainly for economic reasons and childcare as other responsibilities of the household are better taken care by a joint family set up than in a nuclear family and point to the imperative need for supportive services for lessening the burden of household chores and childcare[51].

Pavan Visaria[52] has given a trend report on employment as a review of literature on Indian employment studies. He highlights on the unemployment estimates and the resulting severe economic problems as given by the planning commission during 1955-66. Succeeding Five Year plans had to grapple with increasing dimensions of backlog of unemployment. His survey covered the varied aspects of employment viz., a) concepts and problems of measurement of labour force, employment and underemployment, b) empirical studies of the size of the labour force and participation rates, rural unemployment, underemployment and unemployment in urban areas and educated unemployment, and c) composition of the workers in the labour force in rural and urban sectors.

The conditions of women in India should be pursued with an appropriate approach to comprehend the dynamics of our society in general and place the women in a societal backdrop. Assessed from this angle many felt dissatisfied with the first ever written report on women in India-Towards Equality (GOI, 1974) and Indian Women (GOI, 1975). They no doubt have provided a 'plethora of variables', statistical tables and sample surveys only to give an 'extremely watered down version' of the state of Indian women[53].

Technological innovations, agricultural mechanisation and the introduction of high yielding varieties of crops have had different kinds of impact on women and their allocations of labour. The net result of technology according to some studies is that women have suffered rather than benefited from them in many Asian countries[54].

It is the negative impact of the technology on women that is very apparent. Women of various social classes are pushed out by men despite official acceptance of the pattern of equality. The same is the case with workers with no education and training when they are less in demand: men get a preference over women, and in turn push women of the same category out of employment. The new methods of agriculture are all taught to or learnt by only men. The introduction of western model farm implements had affected the 'daily-wage-work' done by women. This displacement of women from farms adds fuel to fire and in the long run these imbalances would aggregate the hazards to the status of women. The World Bank and the IMF have made certain structural adjustments necessary in the borrower countries like India. These have in turn imposed "severe and discriminatory burden on women in developing countries"[55]. For example, to have the economic efficiency the introduction of appropriate technology in khadi and village industries too has resulted in diversion of labour. Most of the dirty, subordinate, low skill and low paid work goes to women. The technological flexibility of the garment industry despite its capacity to generate employment has lead to subcontracting and the attendant exploitation and subjugation of women at work. To the extent that weaving technology had developed, spinning has not developed to improve the productivity of women.

G.Chandrasekhar Rao (2004)[5657] observed that implications for Gender Equality that focused the Gender gap between men and women in work participation are very high and it varied considerably across many states in the country. The women participation rate at the all India level increased to 39.3 per cent as per the 2001 census from 37.5 per cent according to 1991 census. While the work participation rate for males marginally increased from 51.6 per cent to 51.9 per cent during 1991-2001, for females it improved substantially from 22.7 per cent to 25.7 per cent during the corresponding period. Another important finding of the 2001 census shows a large proportion of female workers engaged in household industries than males both in rural as well as urban areas.

Rohini Banaji (1984), [58] made an attempt to understand the work situation and to make suggestions about women in pharmaceutical and food industries. In their study, "A Challenge for Unions", they found that women are not provided with basic facilities and also there is lack of transport facilities too. Further they work for longer hours and are subjected to discrimination in employment even in recruitment. The study also mentions the negative impact of modern technology in fisherwomen in kerala.

Neera Desai (1987)[59], in the book entitled 'Women and Society in India' emphasised that modern technology can lead to absolute deprivation of women at work by simply eliminating their designated tasks as in textile industry and coal mining or by promoting male substitution as in rice milling and fish processing. They also reviewed a series of studies done on export industries, which reveal that women are employed only for selective tasks. These workers are younger in age, with little education and a majority is casual workers. In the food processing industry women are hired as cheap casual workers in dispersed units often on a piece rate system. Women are employed in this industry mainly in manual processes such as cutting, peeling, packing etc. The author inferred that the emergence of mechanised units has resulted in down grading of women's traditional skill in food processing.

Lalitha Iyer examined the role of women workers in her study on "Overview of employment in the Food and Drink Industries". She interviewed three family production units in the Delhi Food Zone and finds that the situation of the women workers is the same in all of them. She says that their role is not very promising in terms of mobility or position, particularly because the industry is seasonal the women are hired by contractors and women are invariably relegated to doing the lowest level of work with the least skills. As the position of women workers in the food processing industry is inferior, regardless of continuity of service, wages paid are not as per the minimum wages Act. There are no benefits and not even facilities such as toilets, maternity leave, crèches etc. She also noted that usually women are slotted to the occupation, which fetches the least income[60].

Not only in India, but also in most of the European Countries, 50 per cent of the labour force in this industry is women. The evolution of the food processing industries in the West has followed the trend of overall mechanisation, in every sphere of life. She noticed that processing which is a familial function, earlier performed by women of the household has been taken over by the organised industry.

Beena's study on "Technological Change in Women Workers – The Case of Fish Processing Industry in Kerala" reflected on the change that occurred in fish processing industry of Kerala due to advanced technology. The main focus of the study is on the female workforce in this particular industry, which highlighted how technology affected women's employment by comparing the traditional fish processing with that of modern fish processing industry. The observations of the above case study are as follows: There is high concentration of workers in the age group of 15 to 24 years, above 43 per cent of the workers is unmarried. She traced the problems of the women workers in the industry to lack of unionisation among workers. She mentioned that the decentralisation of work and frequent shift in location destroyed the bargaining power of the workers and has resulted in the deterioration of their labour conditions[61].

Mathew's study on Exploitation of Women Labour Employment in Kerala' broadly explained three theoretical aspects of women's employment, emerging trends in the structure of employment in Kerala and in the country and gender-based exploitation of labour under changing environment and institutional framework. The author highlights the process of decentralisation (or informalisation) of production as the first strategy of capital to bypass the social limits imposed by the organised working class to the capitalist exploitation. The most important objective of informalisation was to check the growth of a radical working class movement, which originated in industries such as cashew and coir.[62]

2.3 Studies on Health:

The Joint ILO/WHO Committee on Occupational Health defined occupational health as "The promotion and maintenance of the highest degree of physical, mental and social well-being of workers in all occupations. The prevention among workers of departures from health caused by their working conditions: the protection of workers in their employment from risks resulting from factors adverse to health: the placing and maintenance of the work, in occupational environment adopted to his physiological and psychological equipment and to summarise: the adoption of work to man and of each man to his job"[63].

More women are now working in industries, where the conditions of work are unhygienic and hazardous to their health. Women's employment has bought an improved standard of living and greater financial independence of them on the one hand and many hazards to their health due to hostile environment and exploitation on the other (Kumar)[64].

The World Health Organisation's publication on 'health hazards of human environment' is addressed primarily to health authorities called upon to study environmental problems, although it is hoped that much of it will be of the interest to others concerned with deterioration of the environment. The human environment is considered here as comprising of those external physical, chemical, biological and social influences that have a significant and detectable effect on the health and well being of the individual or on the community of people[65].

The Report of World Health Organisation states that social conditions like housing, crowding, nutrition, mode of transportation, necessity for extra earnings etc., are clearly related to the prevalence of various diseases, body weight, height and even life expectancy. In many regions ambient industrial air pollution is high, thus increasing the total exposure of the workers. There tends to be differences in exposure, even for workers performing the same work, owing to differences in patterns of movement, in experience in handling the work task, in personal cleanliness', etc. There may be a considerable range in personal exposure. This applies not only to chemical exposure, but also to physical workload, heat, noise exposure etc[66].

"The Health Status of Indian Women", prepared by Nasreen Fazalbhoy, has focused attention on the question of women health, since health touches the question of survival itself. To understand the causes of ill health of people, studying a group or a gender is not sufficient. The health status of any group is a dynamic and complex manifestation of social, economic, political, cultural and historical factors. The report contains the issues like the assessment of women's health situation, social determinations of women's health, attitudes regarding health programmes and policies, etc. 'Occupational status and health', is also considered in the study. According to the author, one of major negative effects of the present trend of developmental policies is their impact on the poor. Women have been affected in that mechanisation which has taken over many of the traditional jobs that woman did. Those women have been thrown into the sectors that engage casual labour. She further points out that the kind of jobs available to women are low paid and menial. The report also summarises the nature of women's work and related health problems[67].

Park's book entitled 'Preventive and Social Medicine" contains a Chapter on "Occupational Health". Occupational Health is essential preventive medicine. Both have the same aim – 'the prevention of disease and maintance of the highest degree of physical and social well-being' of workers in all occupations; the levels of application of preventive measures are the same – health promotion, specific protection, early diagnosis and treatment, disability limitation and rehabilitation; the tools are also the same: epidemiological approach, statistics, health screening and health education. Occupational health, therefore, is the application of preventive medicine in all places of employment[68].

SECTION – II

In this Section, an attempt is made to observe the new economic policy on women in export processing zones in India.

2.4 New Economic Policy on Women in the Export Processing Zones:

The New Economic Policy (NEP), announced by the Govt. of India in 1991, as a part of the Structural Adjustment Policy Package, is suggested by the international lending agencies like International Monetary Fund, in order to overcome the severe foreign exchange crisis. NEP is aimed at increasing nation's foreign exchange through liberalised trade polices, such as relaxing taxes on profits and on import of materials and machines, and lifting trade barriers for expanding production. As part of this strategy, Export Processing Zones and 100 per cent Export Oriented Units were established to augment exports and utilising cheap and flexible labour available in the country. The area of liberalisation and deregulation has changed the structure of labour markets, making them increasingly more flexible than in the past. The economic rationality of flexible labour that is employing casual, temporary and contract labour that could be dispensed at will fits well for the strategy that preaches liberalisation and cost-effective production, as it reduces wages and non-wage costs. It in turn reduces the production cost and results in low prices, which is necessary to compete in the world market. In the words of Sudha Deshpande[69]: "It is more difficult to assess the impact of NEP on women's social and economic well-being since this area is yet to be explored. In the absence of comprehensive studies, we need to rely on scanty evidence wherever available and try to guess what is likely to happen to legal and social rights that were sanctioned so far to industrial workers in India".

The New Economic Policy is expected to result in increased employment, but United Nations (1992) observed that this employment growth has been mostly low cost flexible labour (quoted in Sudha Deshpande1993), Bandyopadhyay[70] also says that, even though structural adjustments increased job opportunities for women, the type of employment it generates is low paid jobs and the conditions of work are also bad.

Employment generation is an important objective for EPZs in smaller countries, but may not be so in the case of large economies like India. EPZs help in generating additional employment, but their overall impact depends upon the size of the economy and the stage of its development. In smaller economies, successful EPZs have a significant proportion of workforce in the manufacturing sector. This is true of EPZs in Mauritius, Mexico and the Dominican Republics. In Singapore, Malaysia and Sri Lanka, EPZs employment constitutes a high proportion of overall industrial employment, which ranges between 16 to 35 per cent. In Hong Kong, Mexico, Korea and Taiwan, it is estimated to be between 5 to 6 per cent[71]. EPZ employment is not substantial in India as their number is small and size is modest. However, Chinese Zones have generated considerable employment in view of their large size and broader scope of permitted activities. A United Nations Industrial Development Organisation (UNIDO) study has estimated the employment in the Chinese Zone in 1991 was as high as 2.2 million, out of worldwide EPZ employment of 4 million. Of all the successful economies under reform in the East Asia & Pacific region, China has very close similarities in her economic features with India - her vast size, large population, low per capita income, pre-reform, protected external trade, large dominance of an inefficient public sector and a productive system with obsolete technology.

In the case of smaller economies, employment generation has not been a key EPZ objective in India as the impact of incremental employment is not very significant. An International Labour Organisation (ILO) study has also concluded that while the impact of multinational companies (MNCs) on employment generation and investment in the EPZs was very high in Singapore and Malaysia and significant in Korea and Hong Kong, it is negligible in India[72]. However, considering their number and size, Indian EPZs have generated reasonably satisfactory incremental employment. The size of workforce has gone up from 35,205 in 1990-91 to 81,255 in 1997-98. Santa Cruz Electronics Export Processing Zone (SEEPZ), Mumbai, is the largest employment provided among the zones with 40 per cent. The overall male or female sex ratio is 57.48, though it varies widely from zone to zone. The proportion of female workers is highest in Cochin Export Processing Zone, (CEPZ), Kerala, at 61 per cent, and the lowest in Noida Export Processing Zone (NEPZ), Uttar Pradesh, at 25 per cent.

These variations are essentially on account of the type of industries set up in the respective zones. The proportion of female workers is usually higher in garments and electronic sectors. As garments and textile units are dominant in Madras Export Processing Zone (MEPZ), Chennai, Kandla Free Trade Zone (KFTZ), Gujarat and CEPZ, the proportion of female workers in these zones is higher than in other zones. As on 31.3.2005, there are 811 units in operation in the 8 functional SEZs provide employment to about 100,650 persons out of which 32,185 are female.[73] Number of studies has been carried out on women workers in the SEZs. and that the profile of average worker assists the analysis of the reasons for certain practices which exist in the zones. It has been estimated that approximately 85 per cent of the workforce in the zones are female. that over 50 per cent of that workforce is between the age of 19 and 24. that 60 per cent have attained an educational level of and above the General Certificate in Education (Ordinary level) Examination. 82 per cent of the female workforce is unmarried; with more than 50 per cent stating that their families were economically dependent on them. Nearly, 75 per cent of the survey populations were not residents in or near the SEZs and were thus based in lodgings in the vicinity[74]. Most of the Indian zones are labour intensive; employment generation has been a positive feature of Indian Zones.

Despite all the limitations that a workingwoman faces, every woman must be a worker, contribute to society in a large or small measure. Women have to psychologically prepare themselves to be more effective members of the society. Every woman who has the privilege of education must be willing, if necessary, to share with men the task of shaping society. Then alone will the stigma of dependency attached to her will reduce and it ensures respect and dignity and ultimately enhance the status of women.

2.5 Summary:

An overview of the studies on women and export processing zones in India, though limited in number, has thrown much light on the employment and working conditions of women in these zones. The studies have revealed that the nature of women's employment, downgraded women's skills with the introduction of modern technology. They have also highlighted the strenuous nature of tasks allotted, the poor working conditions, which have adverse implications on their health. They have also sharply focused on the exploitative employment conditions in the SEZs, with low wages and with longer working hours. These studies have also identified the occupational health hazards in the SEZ units.

Thus, a glance at the earlier works in the area is valuable in itself as it identified the problems faced by women on the employment and health aspects. But a majority of these studies are descriptive in nature and some are based on casual observations. There are very few studies with sound empirical data and were subjected to statistical tests to validate the results. Further, in a country like India, with its wide diversity, the need for studies covering different regions assumes significance in evolving location specific and area specific policy framework to suit the widely varying conditions. On this count, studies on the employment and health conditions of women in Special Economic Zones on the East Coast are limited. This provides a strong case for the present Study.

References:

---

[1] I.L.O. (2003): *Women in Changing World*, Geneva.

[2] Government of India (2003): *The Ministry of Labour and Employment*, New Delhi.

[3] Statutory Commission (2003):"Women's Employment in a Changing World" *Women and Economy*, pp.17-32.

[4] Sunder (1981): "Characteristics of Female Employment, Implications of Research and Policy", *Economic and Political Weekly*, May 9th, Vol.XVI, No. 18, Bombay.

[5] *Encyclopedia Britannica*, Vol.19, p.913.

[6] Japan is a combination of Modernity and Tradition. Only recently the socialist Movement has altered the discriminatory practice against women.

[7] UNDP (1991): *Human Development Report*, Oxford University Press, New York, p.35.

[8] Burggrat S.P.U. (1984): "Women, Youth and Minorities and Case of missing Productivity", *American Economic Review*, May p.254.

[9] I.L.O. (1958): "Employment and Occupation", Geneva.

[10] Nath Kamal (1968): "Women in the working force in India", *Economic and Political Weekly*, August, pp.1205-1215.

[11] Ghosh Balasnisikha (1984): "Displacement of the Female in the Indian Labour Force", *Economic and Political Weekly*, June, Vol.XIX, No. 24.

[12] Government of India (2003-04): Economic Survey 2003-04, New Delhi.

[13] Whyte R.O. (1982): *The Rural Women of Asia*, Colorado.

[14] Kapur .P (1970): "*Marriage and Working Women in India*", Delhi

[15] International Labour Organisation (1972):" Employment, Income and Equity, A Strategy for Increasing Productive Unemployment in Kenya", Geneva.

[16] Alam K (1987): *The changing role of women in the rural Economic of Asia*. Conference volume of the Indian Economic Association Seventh Annual Conference, Jaipur.

[17] Jagadish Prasad (1987): "Women in the labourforce: a case study of Bihar, conference volume of the Indian Economic Association, Seventh Annual Conference, Jaipur.

[18] D.R.Godgil (1965): *Women in the working force in India, Kunde data Memorial lecture*, Asian Publishing House, New Delhi, p.27.

[19] Ashok Mitra (1951): *Censes of India*, West Bengal, part-1, p. 526.

[20] J.N.Sinha (1961): *Indian working force* –Its growth changing composition, censes of India.

[21] J.P.Ambannavar, *Employment pattern of India since 1911*.

[22] Planning Commission (*1978*): *Working group on women*, New Delhi.

[23] Government of India (1969), *Report of the National Commission on Labour*, Ministry of Labour, New Delhi.

[24] Tirupati town (1987): PhD thesis, Australian National University, Canberra.

[25] Jayanti (1987): *Role of women in Urban Development. A case study of Tirupati Town*, (Unpublished dissertation), Department of Economics, S.V.University, March.

[26] Singh etal. (1976): Andrea Menifee Singh and A.D.Souze, *The Urban Poor*, Manohar publication, New Delhi.

[27] Manjudar.T (1977): "The urban poor and social change: A case study of squatter settlements in Delhi", *Social Action* 27(3).

[28] A. Singh and A.D.Souze (1976): *Position of women in important basis in Delhi*, ISI Mimeo.

[29] Sulbha Brehme (1979): *Economic plight of Tamil women in Pune*, ICSSR, Mimeo.

[30] Sunder Pushpa (1981): "Characteristic of female employment-implication of Research and Policy", *Economic and Political Weekly*, Vol XVI No.19. May.

[31] Boseup and Ester (1970): *Women's Role in Economic development*, St Martin Press, New York.p.35.

[32] Sukle Bose (1985): "Caste, Trade and female labour participation", *Social Change*, Vol. 15. No. 2.june.

[33] D.Radha Devi and M. Ravinder (1985): "Working women and household work", *Social Change*, Vol. 15. No.2.June.

[34] Ahmed and Karuna (1979): "Studies of Educated Working Women in India-Trends issues", *Economic and Political Weekly*, Vol.XIV, No.33. August.

[35] Ramachandhar P (1964): *Attitudes of women to part-time employment*, Part-1 Report, Department of Social Research, Tata Institute of Social Science, Bombay.

[36] Mahajan, A (1966): "Women's Two Roles; a case study of Role Conflict," *Indian Journal of Social Work*, 24 (4), p.p.

[37] Ashok Mitra (1951): *The status of women, Literacy and employment*, ICSSR, Allied Publisher, p.52.

[38]Usha Kundra (1999): "Employment opportunities for women in changing Society", *Kurukshetra,* Department of Humanities, Regional Engineering College.

[39]Lalitha Devi (1902): *Status and Employment of Women on India*, B.R. Publishing Corporation, Delhi.

[40] Sushma Singhal (1995): *Development of Education Occupation and Employment of Women in India*, Mittal Publication, Delhi.

[41] Government of India (1087): *Department of Rural Development*, Ministry of Agriculture: Annual Report. p.21.

[42] International Labour Office (1982): *Rural Department and Women in Asia*, p.14, Geneva.

[43] Viswanadhan, M. (1994): *Women in Agriculture and Rural development*, Print well, Jaipur, Rajasthan.

[44] P.R. Reddy (1998): *Women in Development,* Vol. 1&2, B.R.Publishing Corporation. Delhi.

[45] Yadav, Y.S. (2000): *Aquaculture and Women Employment,'* Development Commission, Ministry of Agriculture. New Delhi.

[46] Neeta Anand (2003): "Working Women: Issues and Problems" *Yojana*, March, p.11.

[47] Government of India (2001): *Census Report 2001*, New Delhi.

[48] Elson, D. (1981): *The Subordination of Women and the Internationalisation of Factory Production*, Routledge, London.

[49] Gayatri (2002): *Gender, Poverty and Employment in India*, unpublished Paper, ILO, New Delhi.

[50] Duraiswamy P.M. (1997): "Gender Bias in the Scientific and Technical Labour Markets: A Comparative Study of Tamil Nadu and Kerala," Centre for Development Studies, Trivandrum.

[51] Prabhakar, R. (1975): *Study of Hundred – Employed Women in Udaypur,* University of Delhi (Thesis Unpublished).

[52] Visaria, P. (1976), "Employment – A Trend Report: A Survey of Research in Economics", Vol.No.11, *Macro Economics*, Chapter III.

[53] Bogchi, J (1976), "Killed with Kindness", *Economic and Political Weekly*, 24th January, p.101.

[54] Whyte, R.O. (1982): *The Rural Women of Asia*, Colorado.

[55] Afhar, H. (1992):*Women and Adjustment Policies*, London.

[56] Chandrasekhar Rao, G. (2004): "Changing trends in Work Participation rates and Women Employment in India", Paper presented at National Seminar, 30th & 31st December, Department of Economics, Andhra University, Visakhapatnam.

57. Rohini, B. and Sujatha, D. (1984): "Force and Organisational Strategies", *Economic and Political Weekly,* Vol.XXIX, No.18, April 30, pp. WS. 39-48.

58. Desai and Neera (1987): *Women and Society in India*, Ajantha Publications, New Delhi.

59 Lalitha, Iyer, (1990):"Overview of Employment in the Food and Drink Industries", in Divys Pandey & Mira Savara (ed), *'Between the Farm and Thali-Women and Food Processing*, Research Centre for Women Studies, S.N.D.T., Womens University, Mumbai.

[61] Beena, D. (1991):"Technological change and Women Workers: The case of Fish Processing Industry in Kerala", in Chetana Kalbagh (Ed), *Women and Development*, Vol.1, Discovery Publishing House, New Delhi.

[62] Mathew (1991B): "Women and the so-called Informal Sector-Strategies and Counter Strategies", in Chetana Kalbagh (ed), *Women and Development*, Vol. 5, Discovery Publishing House, New Delhi.

[63] W.H.O. (Technical Report Series No. 66), (1953): *Joint ILO/WHO Committee on Occupational Health* (Second Report), Geneva.

[64] .Kumar, R. (1990)." Health of Working Women", in Ram Kumar (Ed), *Women, Health, Development and administration: Principles and Practice,* Vol. 1, Deep and Deep Publications, New Delhi.

[65] W.H.O. (1972): *Health Hazards of Human Environment*, Geneva.

[66] W.H.O. (1973): *Environmental and Health Monitoring in Occupational Health,* Geneva.

[67] Nasreen and Fazalbhoy (1988): *The Health Status of Indian Women*, Unit for Urban Studies, T.I.S.S., Mumbai.

[68] Park, K. (1995): *Park's Text book of Preventive and Social Medicine*, 14th edition, Banarsidas Bhanot Publishers, Jabalpur, India.

[69] Sudha Despande (1993): "Structural Adjustment and Feminisation", in Alkh N. Sharma, Seema Singh (Ed) *Women and Work-Changing scenario in India, Indian Society of Labour Economics*, Patna, B.P Publishing Corporation, New Delhi.P.82.

[70] Bandyopadhyay (1995): "Hunger and Jobless Growth"-Impact of SAP, *Manistream*, May13, p.16.

[71] ILO / UNCTC (1988): *Economic and Social Effects of Multinational Enterprises in Export Processing Zones*, Geneva, ILO, p.5.

[72] Maex and Rudy (1983): *Employment and Multinationals in Asian Export Processing Zones*, ILO, Geneva.

[73] Ministry of Commerce and Industry (2005): Department of Commerce, India.

[74] ILO (1998): *Labour and Social Issues Relating to Export Processing Zones*, Geneva.

CHAPTER-III

CHAPTER - III
SOCIO-ECONOMIC PROFILE OF WOMEN WORKERS IN THE VSEZ

3.1 Introduction:

In this Chapter an attempt is made to study the socio-economic profile of the women workers in the VSEZ. This Chapter is divided into three Sections. Section-I presents the general activities of EPZs and facilities of the VSEZ, Section –II presents the social conditions of the women workers and Section –III presents the economic conditions of the women workers in the VSEZ.

SECTION - I

3.2.1 Activities of EPZs:

Besides developing physical infrastructure, the EPZs provide fiscal and taxation incentives to attract overseas investment. Infrastructural facilities include development of industrial estates, factory premises and development of plots with supportive services and utilities. The major supporting incentives for the EPZs are:

1. Duty free import of capital goods and raw materials.
2. Exemption from central excise duty,
3. Deemed-export benefits on capital goods and raw-material purchased from DTA,
4. Reimbursement of central sales tax on domestic supplies,
5. Tax holiday for any five consecutive years during the first eight years of operation.
6. Unrestricted foray equity participation, and
7. Lease rent concession during the first three years of operation.

The EPZs infrastructure mainly comprises built standard design factory blocks (SDF), sheds and developed plots. The SDFs are mainly utilised for setting up of medium-sized tools electronics, computer software, gems and jewellery, garments and light engineering units. Besides, sector-specific infrastructure for software, jewellery and garment units have been provided in some zones. The central government has already invested Rs. 2,495 million on providing infrastructure and other services. Telecom, transport and postal services, banking facilities, canteen, medical care, security, power, water supply and sewerage are well provided in the zones. Social and economic infrastructure of housing, schools, hospital and recreational facilities in the periphery are provided by the respective State governments. Besides, pollution clearance certification, approval of building plans, registration on small scale and grant of publicity status are given by the state government authorities. However Infrastructural facilities for all these zones are not of uniform quality, with the possible exception of SEEPZ. Other zones have some gap in the physical and supportive infrastructure, public transport and housing facilities are poor in CEPZ. Local transportation, power and water supply services are not up to the mark in FEPZ. Canteen facilities are deficient and water supply is inadequate in MEPZ. Power and telecom services are needed to further strengthen the NEPZ besides the housing facilities. In KFTZ, electricity supply and water supply is inadequate. Public transport and housing facilities are poor in VEPZ.

The EPZs claim to provide a hassle-free environment for day-to-day operation, which is their major strength. Procedures are relatively simple and transparent. An Assistant Commissioner of

Customs who ensures fast clearance of import and export, sub-contracting and sales in the domestic traded area and also takes care of other allied customs matters heads the customs wing. Zones also provide pre-establishment support for expediting statutory approvals and clearances required to be given by the various state government authorities.

Developed infrastructure and other support services, lesser trade union activity, relative insulation from regulatory agencies, a five-year tax holiday, reimbursement of central sales tax, low rentals and availability of ready to use and secure premises and pleasing work environment are the main strengths of EPZs. Besides, EPZs also lend credibility to the foreign buyers. Zones fare very well in so far as physical infrastructure custom facilities, labour relation and procedural cases are concerned. However, the quality of supportive services is, by and large, meager. Zones also come out poorly in regard to availability of manpower and trade finance.

Intercepted power supply and telecom services, inadequate transport and housing infrastructure, cumbersome customs procedures, restrictions on the movement of samples and materials for sub-contracting, unavailable duty structure for DTA sales and inflexible VAT norms have been the main weaknesses of EPZs.

3.2.2 Issues in EPZs:

1. Application of labour laws, maintenance of labour standards and reorganisation of labour rights of employees.

2. For achieving the objective of successful EPZs, especially in a global context of increasing competently, the emphasis has to be an adoption of better technology, improvement in work organisation, development of skills and smooth labour management relations.
3. Restriction of trade union rights either directly or indirectly, lack of enforcement of labour legislation, absence of workers' organisations, lack of effective structure of labour management relations and shortage of human resource development programme.
4. Considering that the bulk of EPZ workers are females, particular emphasis should be laid on an integrated programme of human resource development with components of education, awareness, industrial culture and health, family care, maternity benefits and child care.
5. **Employment**: The benefit of employment generation on the host economies had been highlighted by some studies. Employment generation is an important objective for EPZs in smaller countries. In case of a large economy like India, EPZs have helped in generating additional employment. As such their overall impact depends on the size of the economy and the stage of its development and the size of the zones. Chinese zones have generated considerable employment due to their large size of broader scope of permitted activities. EPZ employment is small and size is modest (About 84,500 employees source: Kundra, 2000 and VEPZ Administration).
6. **Concentration of women workers in EPZs**: A distinctive feature of EPZ is the high proportion of women in the workforce. Employees have shown preference for women workers since it is

believed that sensitivity, patience and other gender-specific attributes make them more suitable than men for carrying out tasks that demand painstaking attention to detail. Women, regardless of their level of education, constitute bulk of the unskilled and semi-skilled workers and this is particularly pronounced in the textile, leather, electronics and gem and jewellery industries.

Women at present constitute 36 per cent of all workers employed in Indian EPZs, although there are wide variations across zones, between sectors and even individual units within each zone. Regional socio-cultural factors and perhaps the higher educational level would be the reasons why the two Southern Zones in Tamil Nadu (MEPZ) and Kerala (KEPZ) have consistently monitored higher proportion of women as compared to other zones. But even such factors have been unable to counter or withstand the broad trend of declining proportion of women working in Indian EPZs from 48 per cent in the early 90's to 36 per cent by 2001. However, it is true that the number of women in the export oriented industries in India, too, has generally been reducing, and it is also true that this sizable presence of women is an indicator of low wages, and poor conditions of work in these industries. The appearance of the declining proportion of women in EPZs points to a saga of callous employee relations which any form of social dialogue must address.

3.2.3 Wages and Labour Standards:

There is an opinion on that besides labour being cheap, wages in the developing countries are kept artificially low by low level of social protection. However, wage rates in EPZs are low only in comparison with international standards. The ILO (1998 a) notes that the minimum wages rates and take-home pay of workers in EPZs are higher than that of workers in similar factories outside.

3.2.4 Labour Laws:

Central governments have passed EPZs legislation that suspends the application of all or some labour laws in the zones. Workers may be prohibited from joining unions engaging in any from of trade union activity. Their prohibition can be for an indefinite period. Apart from EPZs specific laws, there other regulations that make it possible either to restrict trade union membership or related activities, such as initiating industrial action. Enterprises in EPZs may be declared essential services activities, vital to notional interest or pioneer industries in which strikes and other forms of industrial action will be considered illegal.

3.2.5 Public Utility/ Essential Services Status for the Units:

In India, EPZs have been given public utility status under the Industrial Disputes Act 1947 by the respective State governments. In SEZs, the State government may delegate the power of the labour commission to the commissioners posted exclusively.

VSEZ: In the sphere of economic ups and down, the liberalisation policy adopted in the Indian scenario has given way to super-headed competition. Every kind of industry would require great support from the state. Hence, for single-minded growth, the government of India has setup Special Economic Zones for providing a hassle-free environment and high quality infrastructure. Export units are not merely in competition with the domestic counterparts but also with their counterparts in SEZs Worldwide. SEZs play an important role in giving an impact to the free exports. VSEZ offers the best of infrastructure and services, a prospective entrepreneur looks for. Readymade infrastructure, modern support services, and industry-friendly administrative setup are its highlights.

3.2.6 Advantages of the VSEZ:

1. High quality infrastructure at affordable rentals with initial concessions.
2. On-line services for all clearances.
3. Strategically located, easy accessibility to South and South East Asian countries.
4. Strong industrial base and productive workforce.
5. Well connected by rail, road and air links to rest of the country.
6. Readily available skilled workforce at reasonable wages.
7. In-house customs facility for quick and easy clearances.
8. High quality and low cost social infrastructure.

3.2.7 What the SEZ Scheme Offers?

1. SEZ is a designated duty-free enclave and treated as foreign territory for trade operations, duties and tariffs.
2. Units can be set up for manufacturing, trading or service activity.
3. Units have to achieve only positive Net Foreign Exchange (NFE) within three years.
4. Exemption from customs and central excise duty on import\local procurement of capital goods, raw materials, consumable, spares etc.

5. 100 per cent Direct Foreign Investment through automatic route in SEZs and full and free repatriation of export proceeds permitted.
6. Part of production or production process may be undertaken in the domestic area including jewellery units. Sub contracting part of production process is also permitted abroad.

3.2.8 Fiscal Incentives:

1. Exemption of service tax-only to SEZ units in India.
2. Exemption from payment of Central Sales Tax (CST).
3. Complete exemption from payment of Income Tax for the first five years and 50 per cent for the next years.

3.2.9 Exclusive State SEZ Policy:

Policy and incentives offered by state government.

1. All concerned State Governments shall depute an officer to look after permissions/clearances in respect of SEZ units.
2. Self-certification procedure has been introduced for filing of regular returns.
3. Public utility status granted.
4. Women working in night shifts allowed for software units.

3.2.10 Incentives:

1. Exemption from levy of sales tax on the inputs supplied by the units within SEZ and off Zone to the units located in the SEZ.
2. Exemption from payment of stamp duty and registration fee on registration of lease deeds for allotment of plots/SDFs.

3. Exemption from payment of capital contribution charges for supply of water.
4. 50 per cent exemption in payment of development charges for supply of power.

3.2.11 INFRASTRUCTURE:

Infrastructure facilities are given on 15 years renewable lease basis. These facilities are listed below:

3.2.11.1 Facilities:

1. Development of plots and ready-built modules at nominal rental.
2. Abundant supply of quality power and water.
3. Excellent all weather roads, drainage system, lighting etc.
4. State of the art Earth Station for extending connectivity to software centers and IT enabled services.

3.2.11.2 Tariff:

1. Plots: Rs.20/- per Sq. m per year.
2. SDFs: Rs.375/- per Sq. m per year.

3.2.11.3 Concessions in Tariff:

1. PLOTS: 75 per cent, 50 per cent, and 25 per cent for first, second and third years respectively.
2. SDFs: 50 per cent, 40 per cent and 25 per cent for first, second and third years respectively.

SECTION – II

In this Section social conditions of the women workers in the VSEZ are examined.

Women constitute a major chunk of the workforce in the export processing zones but unfortunately their economic importance is not recognised at all. Even though women constitute a major portion of the labour-force in the EPZs, the jobs they do are always unskilled or low-skilled ones. Indian women particularly rural, seldom enjoy the same education and training as men. Most of the industries in the EPZs employing women only are labour intensive ones.

As per various studies, the reasons for employing women in the EPZs units are due to certain inherent qualities possessed by women. These qualities, it is argued, are either physiological (like greater physical resilience) or a result of social conditioning (patience, willingness to undertake long hours of monotonous work, concentration and attention to detail, etc.).[1]

A study conducted in 1997-98 noted that women worked in significant numbers in the garment, footwear and electronics industries in Noida, which were also found to be among the more labour intensive. For while they accounted for just a little over 27 per cent of the industrial units, more than 41 per cent of the workers (men and women) were employed[2].

The vast majority of workers are migrants from rural areas. By 1987, just a year after the NEPZ came into existence, 83 per cent of the workers of Noida are migrants[3]. An attempt is made in the present Study to examine the social economic conditions of the women workers in the four units of the VSEZ, namely World Wide Diamond (WWD), Madras Knitwear Pvt.Ltd. (MKW), Bangalore Swatters (BSW) and L.I.D. Jewellery Pvt.Ltd (LID)

3.3 Age:

The age of the worker may influence his or her working and production capacity. Age forms one of the important determinant factors in understanding the perceptions, attitudes and capacity of the workers. A majority of earlier studies showed the presence of higher proportion of workers aged 25 years. Surinder Jetley (1990)[4] reported that more than half of the workers in a study conducted on women in food processing industry are aged below 35 years. Vijay, Rukmini Rao and Subha Hussain (1991)[5] on working women in fish processing and other export processing plants also reported that the workers mainly are under the age of 25 years.

In the present Study, data pertaining to the age of women workers in four selected units of VSEZ had been collected. The age in number of years had been grouped into five categories. Against these, the four units' data are presented in Table 3.1.

In four units together, 21-25 years age group women workers account for 52.41 per cent followed by 26-30 years age group, which accounts for 21.87 per cent and 19.29 per cent of women workers are below the age group of 20 years. Among the 311 respondents 31-35 years age group are only 5.79 per cent and a negligible 0.64 per cent are above 36 years age group. The data thus indicates 21-25 years age group is the more potential work group. However, the VSEZ units are showing their work force less than the 30 years age group.

TABLE- 3.1

Age of Women Workers in the VSEZ Units

S. No	Age in Years	VSEZ Units					Per cent
		WWD	MKW	BSW	LID	Total	
1	< 20	03 (5.00)	14 (23.33)	14 (23.33)	29 (48.33)	60	19.29
2	21 – 25	42 (25.77)	31 (19.02)	28 (17.18)	62 (38.04)	163	52.41
3	26 – 30	42 (61.76)	06 (8.82)	10 (14.71)	10 (14.71)	68	21.87
4	31 – 35	14 (77.78)	01 (5.56)	01 (5.56)	02 (11.11)	18	5.79
5	> 36	02 (100.00)	0	0	0	02	0.64
	Total	103	52	53	103	311	
	Per cent	33.12	16.72	17.04	33.12		100.00

Note: Figures in the parenthesis indicate percentages

Source: Data collected from the office of the VSEZ, Visakhapatnam.

As shown ante italics.

Among the four units of the VSEZ, less than 20 years age group are seen in L.I.D. Jewellery Pvt.Ltd (LID) (48.33 per cent), Bangalore Swatters (BSW) (23.33 per cent) and Madras Knitwear Pvt.Ltd. (MKW) (23.33 per cent), while World Wide Diamond (WWD) is shows that higher percentage (77.78) belong to 31-35 age group. The data clearly indicates a divide among the four units, where WWD is distinct by showing workers in all age groups ascending from 20 to 36 years of age, while the remaining three (MKW, VSW and LID) are showing ascending distribution from 20 to 35 years age group.

Therefore, it is inferred that the WWD is extending employment to wider age groups of women than the remaining three units where these units show younger women.

The preponderance of young female workers in EPZs has raised many social issues, which have been the subject matter of intense academic debate. These relate to their working conditions, wage rates and other fringe benefits. It is generally believed that wage rates for female workers are lower than male workers and the hours of work are longer than the norm in industrial countries.[6]

3.4 Marital Status:

The data related to the marital status of the women workers of the four units of the VSEZ is collected in order to understand the nature of social obligations and economic responsibilities. As the data on the age of the workers has categorically shown the younger nature of the women work force in the VSEZ, it is expected that most of them might be unmarried. As expected Table - 3.2 shows that nearly 60 per cent of the women workers are unmarried followed by married, which accounts for 36.66 per cent. A very low percent of 3.52 are divorcee women. These three categories are showing a different trend when the data are computed against the four selected units.

TABLE- 3.2

Marital Status of Women Workers in the VSEZ Units

S. No	Marital Status	VSEZ Units					Per cent
		WWD	MKW	BSW	LID	Total	
1	Un-Married	47 (25.27)	29 (15.59)	33 (17.74)	77 (41.40)	186	59.81
2	Married	53 (46.49)	21 (18.42)	17 (14.91)	23 (20.18)	114	36.66
3	Divorcee	03 (27.27)	02 (18.18)	03 (27.27)	03 (27.27)	11	3.53
	Total	103	52	53	103	311	
	Per cent	33.12	16.72	17.04	33.12		100.00

Note: Figures in the parenthesis indicate percentages

Among the married workers WWD is showing higher percentage (46.49), while LID is showing (41.4per cent) unmarried women. The divorcees are distributed more or less evenly in all the four units. The MKW and BSW units are lying between WWD and LID as far as the marital status of the women workers is concerned. It is inferred that the marital status do not show any significant trend except that married women are more in one unit (WWD) and unmarried women in the other (LID).

The distribution of marital status of these women workers shows the predominance of unmarried workers. The study corroborates with earlier studies, Sharmila Peiris & S.Ranaraja (2001)[7], which reported that 82 per cent of the female workforce is unmarried in EPZs in India. Another study by Nirmala Banerjee (1991)[8] on prawn industry in West Bengal also showed that one-third of the respondents are unmarried

3.5 Education:

In recent years education is recognised as one of the important components of human resource development. In view of this, Government of India has undertaken a number of measures to promote literacy levels. The personality of individuals is developed by their educational status. The level of education also shapes the attitudes, opinions and working capacities.

TABLE- 3.3

Education of Women Workers in the VSEZ Units

S. No	Education	VSEZ Units					Per cent
		WWD	MKW	BSW	LID	Total	
1	<10th Standard	63 (43.45)	18 (12.41)	15 (10.34)	49 (33.79)	145	46.62
2	Intermediate	19 (24.05)	15 (18.99)	22 (27.85)	23 (29.11)	79	25.40
3	Degree	08 (21.05)	07 (18.42)	08 (21.05)	15 (39.47)	38	12.22
4	Diploma	0	07 (53.85)	02 (15.38)	04 (30.77)	13	4.18
5	Technical-ITI	11 (34.38)	05 (15.63)	05 (15.63)	11 (34.38)	32	10.29
6	Others	02 (50.00)	0	01 (25.00)	01 (25.00)	04	1.29
	Total	103	52	53	103	311	
	Per cent	33.12	16.72	17.04	33.12		100.00

Note: Figures in the parenthesis indicate percentages

The data relating to the educational background of the women workers is collected and is grouped into six categories and the same has been presented in the Table 3.3. Among the total sample women workers 46.62 per cent are either tenth standard or less than that. About 25 per cent had education up to intermediate followed by 12.22 per cent who are graduates. The remaining three categories technical, diploma and other account for 10.29 per cent, 4.18 per cent and 1.29 per cent respectively.

The data of the Table clearly indicates that no specific educational requirement is essential except that about 10 years of schooling seems to be the basic qualification to enter into the VSEZ. The education parameter is clearly showing a distinction between WWD and LID where the more number of employees had ten years of schooling in WWD and fifteen years of schooling in LID. The MKM and BSW are sliced between WWD and LID sharing average distribution in the first three categories of education with a clear distinction of preferring candidates with technical background – IIT and diploma holders. The intermediate qualification category is showing more or less equitable distribution among the four units of the VSEZ.

The sample workers are perhaps not quite typical of the average women industrial workers of India. Nirmala Banerjee (1991) summarizes the situation that in most of the non-traditional industries, expanding in urban areas, it was not surprising, that the general educational standards among women were improving. Similar conclusions are found in other studies (Beena, 1991[9], Neera Desai, 1990A[10], Lalitha Iyer, 1990)[11]. All these studies, based on processing industries, reveal that women in modern occupations are more literate than traditional occupations.

3.6 Language:

Language is one medium of communication. Knowing more than one language helps the individual in better communication thereby making them more knowledgeable. The information related to the languages known to the women workers of the VSEZ is collected and the same is presented in Table 3.4.

TABLE- 3.4

Languages known to Women Workers in the VSEZ Units

S. No	Languages	VSEZ Units					Per cent
		WWD	MKW	BSW	LID	Total	
1	Monolingual	61 (35.26)	27 (15.61)	32 (18.50)	53 (30.64)	173	55.63
2	Bilingual	10 (23.81)	13 (30.95)	07 (16.67)	12 (28.57)	42	13.50
3	Trilingual	26 (31.33)	12 (14.46)	13 (15.66)	32 (38.55)	83	26.69
4	Others	06 (46.15)	0	01 (7.69)	06 (46.15)	13	4.18
	Total	103	52	53	103	311	
	Per cent	33.12	16.72	17.04	33.12		100.00

Note: Figures in the parenthesis indicate percentages

The data is grouped into four categories such as Monolingual, Bilingual, Trilingual and others. Among the 311 respondents 55.63 per cent are monolingual, which means they know only their mother tongue. The bi-lingual sample accounts for only 13.50 per cent, while the tri-lingual sample is about 27 per cent. The higher percentages of monolinguals are seen in WWD (35.26 per cent) followed by LID (30.64 per cent). Bilinguals are seen mostly in MKM, whereas Trilingual are seen in LID (38.55 per cent) followed by WWD (31.33 per cent). It is clear from the analyses that more number of monolinguals is seen in WWD, bilingual in MKM and trilingual in LID.

3.7 Community:

In the traditional Indian society, social community forms an important determinant in choosing one's occupation. Social community (caste) is one of the characteristics of the households that specify the social position in the society. The modern industrial scenario to some extent is reducing the social community barriers.

TABLE- 3.5

Social Community of Women Workers in the VSEZ Units

S. No	Social Community	VSEZ Units					Per cent
		WWD	MKW	BSW	LID	Total	
1	OC	48 (41.02)	21 (17.95)	20 (17.09)	28 (23.93)	117	37.62
2	BC	44 (27.33)	23 (14.29)	25 (15.53)	69 (42.86)	161	51.77
3	SC	11 (33.33)	08 (24.24)	08 (24.24)	06 (18.18)	33	10.61
	Total	103	52	53	103	311	
	Per cent	33.12	16.72	17.04	33.12		100.00

Note: Figures in the parenthesis indicate percentages

The data related to the social community of the sampled workers is presented in Table 3.5. The caste groups of these workers is further grouped into three categories such as forward caste (open competition – OC), backward class (BC) and schedule castes (SC). The data on social communities reveals that majority of the respondents (51.77 per cent) belongs to BC group, 37.62 per cent belong to OC group and only 10.61 per cent belong to SC group. The unit wise distribution of workers against their social background has shown that more number of women workers belong to OC group in WWD unit, more number of women workers belong to BC group in LID. The workers belong to SC group are seen in all the four units with even distribution. The MKW and BSW units are different from the rest of WWD and LID units by moderate distribution of OC, BC and SC group workers.

These findings are substantiated by a few other studies. Beena (1991)[12] states that with the exception of a few forward community women, all of them belong to either scheduled castes or backward caste communities. In contrast, another study conducted by Mathew (1991A)[13], on Exploitation of Women Labour Employment in Kerala," mentioned how forward caste women entered the fishing industry. He says traditional industries such as peeling of cashew, coir spinning and processing are considered as 'inferior' occupations in which women of forward castes were rarely engaged. But the commercialisation of agriculture and pauperisation caused by the disappearance of the traditional avenues of employment caused the flow of more and more women belonging to higher communities into these occupations.

3.8 Religion:

The diversity of India is also known through the number of religions. Though India is considered as the land of Hinduism, several religions are harmoniously co-existing. In the traditional Indian Society, caste forms an important determinant in choosing one's occupation. But the modern industrial scenario is reducing the caste barriers. The data related to the religious background of the women working in the four selected units of the VSEZ are collected and presented in Table 3.6.

TABLE-3.6

Religious Background of Women Workers in the VSEZ Units

S. No	Religion	VSEZ Units					Per cent
		WWD	MKW	BSW	LID	Total	
1	Hinduism	87 (34.25)	41 (16.14)	41 (16.14)	85 (33.46)	254	81.67
2	Christianity	12 (26.67)	10 (22.22)	11 (24.44)	12 (26.67)	45	14.47
3	Islamism	04 (33.33)	01 (8.33)	01 (8.33)	06 (50.00)	12	3.86
	Total	103	52	53	103	311	
	Per cent	33.12	16.72	17.04	33.12		100.00

Note: Figures in the parenthesis indicate percentages

The Table indicates about 82 per cent of women workers are Hindus and follow Hinduism as their religion. Among the remaining workers 14.47 per cent follow Christianity and 3.86 per cent Islamism as their religions. The data do not show any pattern among the four units except that Islam following workers is mostly seen in LID and WWD.

3.9 Family Size:

Though the joint family system is a characteristic feature of Hindu society, due to various socio-cultural, political and economic reasons the traditional joint family system is breaking away there by giving rise to nuclear families. At present most of the families in the Indian society are nuclear types.

TABLE-3.7

Family Size of Women Workers in the VSEZ Units

S. No	Number of Persons	VSEZ Units					Per cent
		WWD	MKW	BSW	LID	Total	
1	Two	12 (26.09)	13 (26.26)	10 (21.74)	11 (23.91)	46	14.79
2	Three	30 (37.04)	16 (19.75)	14 (17.28)	21 (25.93)	81	26.05
3	Four	42 (43.30)	16 (16.49)	19 (19.59)	20 (20.62)	97	31.19
4	Five	18 (22.22)	07 (8.64)	09 (11.11)	47 (58.02)	81	26.05
5	Six	01 (16.67)	0	01 (16.67)	04 (66.67)	06	1.92
	Total	103	52	53	103	311	
	Per cent	33.12	16.72	17.04	33.12		100.00

Note: Figures in the parenthesis indicate percentages

The size of the family of the sampled women workers is estimated by number of persons in their families. The families with four members are higher in the sample, which account for 31.19 percent. The families with three and five members are accounting have only two persons. A very negligible percent of 1.92 have six members in their family. It is clear from the analyses that the size of the family is 4 ±1 members.

It is further observed from the Table that the four member families are more in WWD while 5 member families are more in LID. The MKW and BSW units are showing more number of two member families. It is inferred from this analyses that large sized families are more in WWD and LID whereas typical nuclear families are seen in MKW and BSW.

3.10 Dependents:

The economic well being of the family has some relationship with the number of dependants and earners have a positive impact while number of dependants has a negative impact on the economic status of a family.

TABLE-3.8

Dependents on the Family of Women Workers in the VSEZ Units

S. No	Number of Persons	VSEZ Units					Per cent
		WWD	MKW	BSW	LID	Total	
1	One	42 (38.53)	23 (21.10)	18 (16.51)	26 (23.85)	109	42.25
2	Two	33 (33.33)	11 (11.11)	22 (22.22)	33 (33.33)	99	38.37
3	Three	09 (20.00)	04 (8.89)	0	32 (71.11)	45	17.44
4	Four	01 (20.00)	0	01 (20.00)	03 (60.00)	05	1.94
	Total	85	38	41	94	258	
	Per cent	32.95	14.73	15.89	36.43		100.00

Note: Figures in the parenthesis indicate percentages

Based on this assumption the data related to the number of dependants at family level (women worker) is collected and presented in Table 3.8.

Out of 311 sampled women workers only 258 women (families) had dependant members. Single individual dependent women workers are high among their families, which account for 42.25 per cent followed by 38.37 per cent of families who had two dependent persons. Three dependent persons are seen among 17.44 per cent of families. The analysis indicates most of the families had one or two dependents. At unit level one to two individual dependants are more in WWD while two, three and four dependents are more in LID. Among the families of MKW and BSW the number of dependants are one (21.10 per cent) and two (22.22 per cent) respectively. The analyses categorically presents more number of families had more number of dependents in WWD and LID than the MKW and BSW units.

3.11 Decision Making:

The decision-making by women regarding various domestic aspects is an indication of economic empowerment of women in the society. The data pertaining to the decision-making at the family level of the women workers had been gathered to understand the pattern of women empowerment. As the sampled women are either a daughter of a father or wife of a husband, the decision makers would be father, husband or both.

TABLE-3.9

Decision Making in Families of Women Workers in the VSEZ Units

S. No	Decision makers	VSEZ Units					Per cent
		WWD	MKW	BSW	LID	Total	
1	Father	45 (26.47)	25 (14.71)	30 (17.65)	70 (41.18)	170	54.66
2	Husband	08 (34.78)	03 (13.04)	03 (13.04)	09 (39.13)	23	7.39
3	Both	48 (47.52)	18 (17.82)	15 (14.85)	20 (19.80)	101	32.48
4	Others	02 (11.76)	06 (35.29)	05 (29.41)	04 (23.53)	17	5.47
	Total	103	52	53	103	311	
	Per cent	33.12	16.72	17.04	33.12		100.00

Note: Figures in the parenthesis indicate percentages

The distribution of the collected data (Table 3.9) indicates that the decisions in the majority of the families are taken by fathers (54.66 per cent), husbands (7.39 per cent) and both father and husband (32.48 per cent). Only 5.47 per cent of women workers are taking independent decisions (by self) at their family level.

The unit wise distribution of data on decision-making at family level indicates clear distinction among the four units of VSEZ. In the case of WWD 47.52 per cent of families are showing that both father and husband take the decisions whereas in LID fathers (41.18 per cent) are taking decisions followed by husbands (39.13 per cent). Independent decision taking families are seen in MKW (35.29per cent) and BSW (29.41per cent).

SECTION -III

In this Section the economic conditions of the women workers are examined.

Sharma and Sengupta's (1984)[14] study on Women Employment at Santacruaz Electronic Export Processing Zone (SEEPZ), Bumbay showed that one-third of the family income was contributed by the respondents. In another study, conducted by Hussain (1991)[15], the interviewed women contributed more than 50 per cent of the family income. These studies show that almost all women workers in export based industries are from fairly poor families, where their earnings are essential to their families' survival. In this sense, women are by no means supplementary earners; rather their earnings are crucial to their families' survival. This is also corroborated by the findings of the study.

3.12 Personal Income:

The data related to earnings of selected women workers in the sampled units of the VSEZ is grouped into five categories and their respective data are presented in Table 3.10. It is inferred from the Table that 32.48 per cent of women workers fall in the category of less than Rs.2, 000/- income per month followed by 28.62 per cent in 2001-3000 group, then 21.86 per cent in 3001-4000 group, and 12.86 per cent in 4001-5000 group. Only 4.18 per cent of women workers are drawing more than rupees Rs.5, 000/- per month. It is further observed from the Table that more than 60 per cent of the women workers are drawing the salary/wages less than Rs.3000/-.

TABLE-3.10

Average Monthly Income of Women Workers in the VSEZ Units

S. No	Income (in Rupees p.m)	VSEZ Units					Per cent
		WWD	MKW	BSW	LID	Total	
1	< 2000	10 (9.90)	22 (21.78)	18 (17.82)	51 (50.50)	101	32.48
2	2001–3000	24 (26.97)	19 (21.35)	16 (17.98)	30 (33.71)	89	28.62
3	3001–4000	31 (45.59)	08 (11.76)	13 (19.12)	16 (23.53)	68	21.86
4	4001–5000	29 (72.50)	03 (7.50)	04 (10.00)	04 (10.00)	40	12.86
5	> 5001	09 (69.23)	0	02 (15.38)	02 (15.38)	13	4.18
	Total	103	52	53	103	311	
	Per cent	33.12	16.72	17.04	33.12		100.00

Note: Figures in the parenthesis indicate percentages

The unit wise data of the earnings of women workers is showing a clear-cut variation between WWD and LID, where higher wages/salary drawing women are more in the former while in the later; less salary/wages drawing women are more. The women working in MKW and BSW do not show any specific pattern unlike WWD and LID, but none of the women fall in first three categories which falls below Rs.4,000/- per month. It is further observed that only about 17 per cent of the women are drawing more than Rs.4,000/- per month.

3.13 Family Income

The data pertaining to the informant's family income is also sorted out in order to analyze the economic status of women workers at family level. The data related to this parameter is grouped into four categories and the same has been presented in Table 3.11.

TABLE-3.11

Average Family Income of Women Workers in the VSEZ Units

S. No	Income (in Rupees p.m)	VSEZ Units					Per cent
		WWD	MKW	BSW	LID	Total	
1	2001 – 4000	03 (6.98)	10 (23.26)	08 (18.60)	22 (51.16)	43	13.83
2	4001 – 6000	22 (17.32)	26 (20.47)	26 (20.47)	53 (41.73)	127	40.84
3	6001 – 8000	48 (46.60)	16 (15.53)	15 (14.56)	24 (23.30)	103	33.11
4	> 8001	30 (78.95)	0	04 (10.53)	04 (10.53)	38	12.22
	Total	103	52	53	103	311	
	Per cent	33.12	16.72	17.04	33.12		100.00

Note: Figures in the parenthesis indicate percentages

On an average most of the families (73.95 per cent) fall under two categories, such as Rs.4, 000/- to Rs.6, 000/- (40.84per cent) and Rs.6001/- to Rs.8000/- (33.11per cent). A very low per cent of 12.22 families had the higher income range (>Rs.8, 000/-) at the same time 13.83 per cent of families fall in Rs.2001/- to Rs.4000/- group.

The unit wise analysis clearly presents distinction between WWD, LID and the remaining two units (MKW and BSW). The category wise percentage of family incomes showing ascending nature from category one to category four in case of WWD, but the families of LID are showing descending trend from category one to four. The MKW is represented only in three categories with descending trend while BSW is represented in all four categories with a higher percentage in category of the income levels of women workers (2.10 per cent) and their families together (3.11 per cent), the economic well-being is sound in case of WWD and on a moderate footing in LID, while MKW and BSW are lingering between WWD and LID to make economically sound and viable incomes.

3.14 Income –Expenditure (Consumption) Relationship:

Keynes, Duesenberry and Engle widely discussed the relationship between income and expenditure of the households in economic literature. In fact, the relationship between income and expenditure on food and non-food items has assumed much more importance in the thinking of many economists. Engle's hypothesis regarding income-consumption relationship (popularly known as Engle's law) is "as income of a family increases, the proportion of its income spent on necessities such as food falls and that spent on luxuries (consisting of industrial goods and services) increases. In short, it is postulated that the share of expenditure on food decline with the rise in income of the families. Against this backdrop of Engle's hypothesis, the income-consumption relationship of the sample household is analysed. Engle's hypothesis can be tested with the help of temporal analysis or cross-section analysis. As the present Study refers to a single point of time, cross-section analysis is attempted.

3.15 Expenditure on Food Items:

A cross section comparison of income and food expenditure of different groups shows changes in the consumption pattern.

TABLE-3.12

Expenditure on Food Items (per month) of Women Workers in the VSEZ

S. No	Expenditure (in Rupees p.m)	VSEZ Units					Per cent
		WWD	MKW	BSW	LID	Total	
1	< 2000	16 (24.62)	14 (21.54)	10 (15.38)	25 (38.46)	65	20.90
2	2001 – 2500	02 (3.51)	09 (15.79)	09 (15.79)	37 (64.91)	57	18.33
3	2501 – 3000	32 (41.56)	17 (22.08)	15 (19.48)	13 (16.88)	77	24.76
4	3001 – 3500	12 (24.49)	07 (14.29)	11 (22.45)	19 (38.78)	49	15.76
5	3501 – 4000	31 (67.39)	04 (8.70)	05 (10.87)	06 (13.04)	46	14.79
6	4001 – 4500	04 (50.00)	01 (12.50)	01 (12.50)	02 (25.00)	08	2.57
7	4501 – 5000	06 (66.67)	0	02 (22.22)	01 (11.11)	09	2.89
	Total	103	52	53	103	311	
	Per cent	33.12	16.72	17.04	33.12		100.00

Note: Figures in the parenthesis indicate percentages

There is a decline in the share of food expenditure as the income-size increases indicating an inverse relationship between income and share of food expenditure. This phenomenon is more striking in the present Study. (Table-3.12)

The Table shows the expenditure of the respondents on the food items per month. It is observed from the Table that nearly 25 per cent of the respondents are spending Rs.2500-3000 per month. Nearly 25 per cent of the families are spending less than Rs.2,000. And 18.33 per cent, 15.76 per cent and 14.79 per cent of the families are spending between Rs.2001-2500, 3001-3500 and 3501-4000 respectively. On the whole only above 5 per cent of the families are the spending more than Rs.4. 000 on food items. Nearly 95 per cent of the families are spending below Rs.4,000. Which indicates that on the whole the expenditure on food items is low.

3.16 Expenditure on Non-Food Items:

Table 3.13 shows expenditure of the respondents on non-food items. Of the total respondents, 37 per cent are spending between Rs.1000-1500 on non-food items, 29.26 per cent, 21.22 per cent and 5.29 per cent of the respondents are spending Rs.1501-2000, below Rs.1000 and Rs.2001-2500 respectively.

TABLE-3.13

Expenditure on Non-Food Items of Women Workers in the VSEZ Units

S. No	Expenditure (in Rupees p.m)	VSEZ Units					Per cent
		WWD	MKW	BSW	LID	Total	
1	< 1000	06 (9.09)	11 (16.67)	11 (16.67)	38 (57.58)	66	21.22
2	1001– 1500	26 (22.61)	24 (20.87)	20 (17.39)	45 (39.13)	115	36.98
3	1501– 2000	41 (45.05)	14 (15.38)	21 (23.08)	15 (16.48)	91	29.26
4	2001– 2500	11 (61.11)	03 (16.67)	0	04 (22.22)	18	5.79
5	2501– 3000	16 (88.89)	0	01 (5.56)	01 (5.56)	18	5.79
6	>3001	03 (100.00)	0	0	0	03	0.96
	Total	103	52	53	103	311	
	Per cent	33.12	16.72	17.04	33.12		100.00

Note: Figures in the parenthesis indicate percentages

3.17 Savings:

In economic analyses, the income and expenditure go hand in hand not only in assessing the well being but also in estimating the savings, there by showing the economic assets at family level. With this assumption the data related to expenditure (on food and non-food) and savings are sought from the informants. The expenditure on food items inclusive of spending on all edible items is used to know the expenditure per month, and the same has been categorised into seven groups which ranges from less than Rs.2,000/- to Rs.5,000/-. This data is presented against the selected units and the same has been presented in Table 3.14.

TABLE-3.14

Savings (per month) of Women Workers in the VSEZ Units

S. No	Savings (in Rupees p.m)	VSEZ Units					Per cent
		WWD	MKW	BSW	LID	Total	
1	< 500	07 (30.43)	06 (26.09)	04 (17.39)	06 (26.09)	23	9.06
2	501 – 1000	19 (26.39)	12 (16.67)	17 (23.61)	24 (33.33)	72	28.34
3	1001–1500	09 (25.00)	02 (5.56)	07 (19.44)	18 (50.00)	36	14.17
4	1501–2000	15 (28.30)	11 (20.75)	04 (7.55)	23 (43.40)	53	20.87
5	> 2001	39 (55.71)	08 (11.43)	12 (17.14)	11 (15.71)	70	27.56
	Total	89	39	44	82	254	
	Per cent	35.05	15.35	17.32	32.28		100.00

Note: Figures in the parenthesis indicate percentages

Table 3.14 shows that the savings of women respondents per month in the VSEZ units. It is observed that 78 per cent of the responds are saving from Rs.500-1000, followed by 27.56 per cent are saving above Rs.2,000 per month. Nearly 35 per cent of the respondents are saving between RS.1000-2000 per month. Among units of the VSEZ the proportion of savings of WWD unit is highest to the per cent of 35.05, followed by LID (32.28 per cent), BSW (17.32 per cent) and MKW (15.35 per cent).

3.18 Source of Income:

The distribution of the workers according to families with other source of income is presented in Table 3.15.

TABLE-3.15

Sources of Income of Women Workers in the VSEZ Units

S. No	Sources	VSEZ Units					Per cent
		WWD	MKW	BSW	LID	Total	
1	House Rents	07 (33.33)	04 (19.05)	02 (9.52)	08 (38.10)	21	6.75
2	Tailoring	17 (39.53)	05 (11.63)	04 (9.30)	17 (39.53)	43	13.83
3	Agriculture	03 (23.08)	05 (38.46)	02 (15.38)	13 (23.08)	13	4.18
4	Others	11 (36.67)	04 (13.33)	08 (26.67)	07 (23.33)	30	9.65
5	Primary (VSEZ)	65 (31.86)	34 (16.67)	37 (18.14)	68 (33.33)	204	65.59
	Total	103	52	53	103	311	
	Per cent	33.12	16.72	17.04	33.12		100.00

Note: Figures in the parenthesis indicate percentages

The distributions of workers according to families with other sources of income are presented in Table 3.15. A few families (34.41 per cent) have other sources of income. A substantial proportion (13.83 per cent) of families is obtaining income through tailoring. But more than 65 per cent of the families are depending on their earnings without any other source of income.

3.19 Summary:

To conclude, traditionally Indian women were involved in household work and reproduction of children. However, in recent times due to financial constraints and due to changing attitudes, women have to work outside their home to earn a living. The attitude in the society has not changed completely as men seldom do the household work. Women work outside and when they come home, they have to do the domestic work too. After independence, the Government of India provided for specific constitutional guarantees to enhance the status of women. Such guarantees are to be given without any discrimination on the basis of religion, race, caste, sex or place of birth. Despite these safeguards and guarantees, women's status still appears to be mostly confined to traditional house-hold activities such as cooking, cleaning, washing, child rearing, etc. However in recent years involvement of women seems to be increasing outside the arena of traditional household activities. It was seen in the women of all the four units in the VSEZ.

The VSEZ mainly employs young unmarried women. Most of them belong to Hindu religion and more are from the backward community. All are literate and it signifies the changing trend of urban industrial working women. The family background of the respondents shows that the workers belong to nuclear families. The occupations of the head of the household shows that neither they are engaged in prestigious occupations nor minimal jobs. Half of the samples workers play a major role in decision-making regarding family expenditure. Finally, it can be concluded that the women workers working in these units are having low socio-economic background.

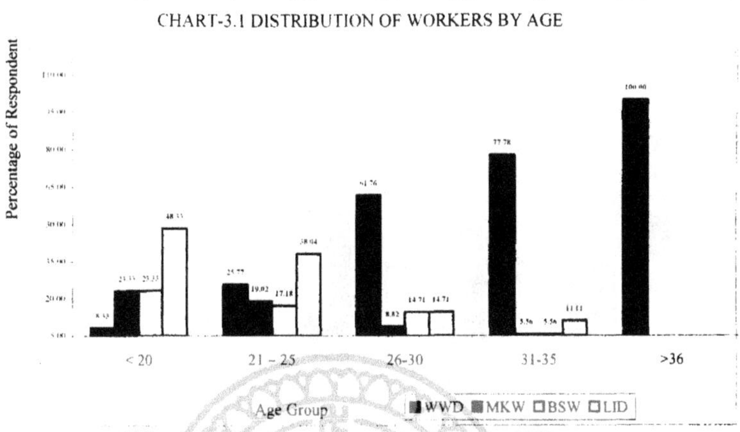
CHART-3.1 DISTRIBUTION OF WORKERS BY AGE
Percentage of Respondent
< 20
21 – 25
26-30
31-35
>36
Age Group
WWD MKW BSW LID

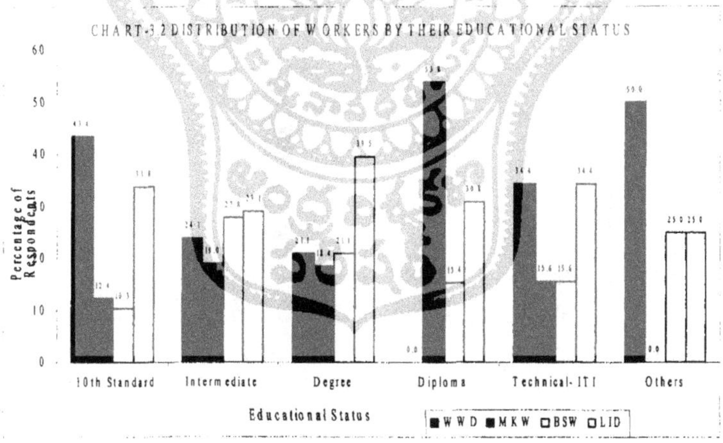
CHART-3.2 DISTRIBUTION OF WORKERS BY THEIR EDUCATIONAL STATUS
Percentage of Respondents
10th Standard
Intermediate
Degree
Diploma
Technical- ITI
Others
Educational Status
WWD MKW BSW LID

CHART-3.3 DISTRIBUTION OF WORKERS BY FAMILY SIZE

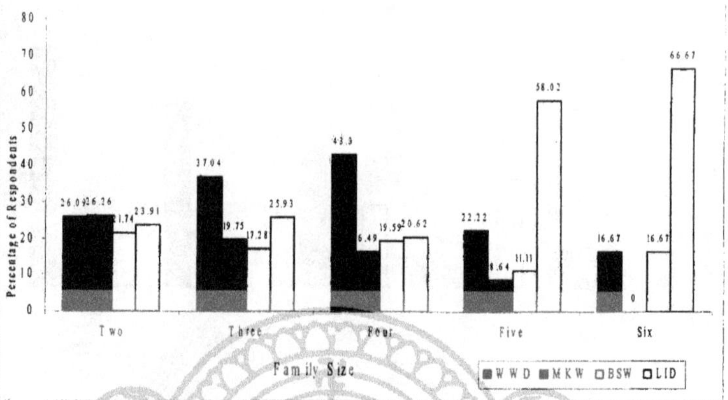

CHART-3.4 DISTRIBUTION OF WOMEN WORKERS BY DECISION MAKING

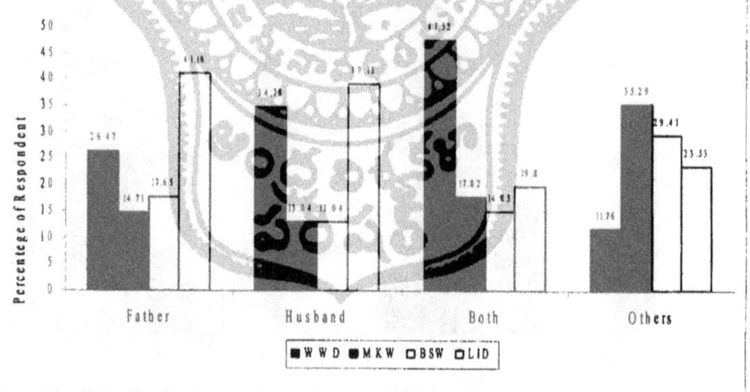

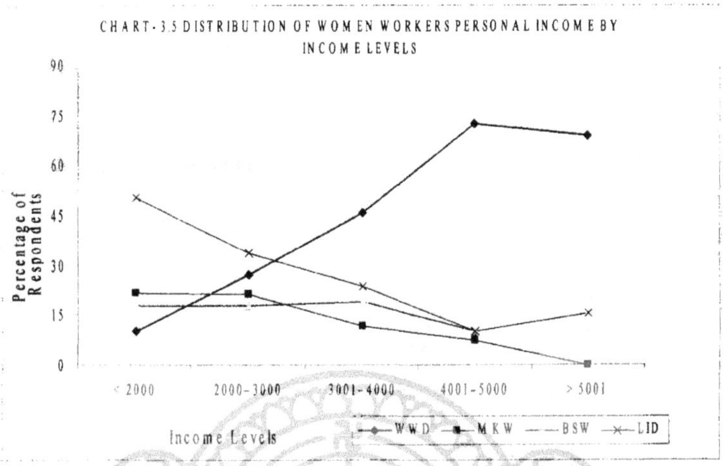

CHART-3.5 DISTRIBUTION OF WOMEN WORKERS PERSONAL INCOME BY INCOME LEVELS

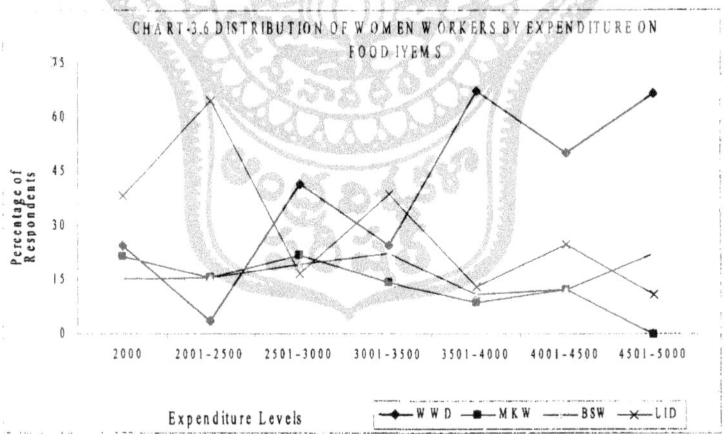

CHART-3.6 DISTRIBUTION OF WOMEN WORKERS BY EXPENDITURE ON FOOD IYEMS

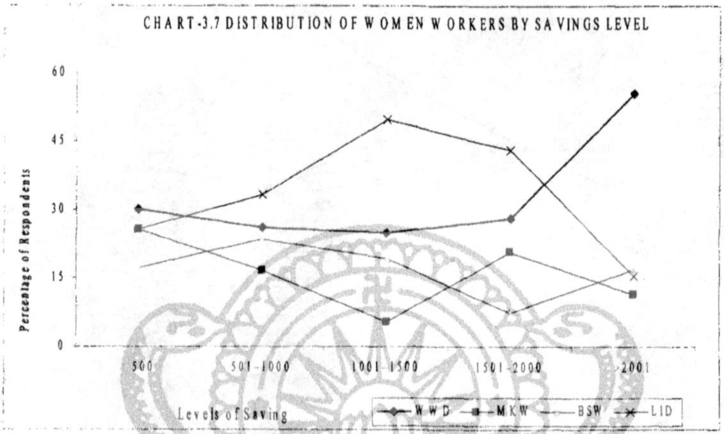
CHART-3.7 DISTRIBUTION OF WOMEN WORKERS BY SAVINGS LEVEL
Percentage of Respondents
60
45
30
15
0
500
501-1000
1001-1500
1501-2000
>2001
Levels of Saving
WWD
MKW
BSW
LID

References:

[1] Rajiv Kumar (1998): *India's Export Processing Zones,* Oxford University Press, India.

[2] Centre for Women's Development Studies (CWDS) (1997): *Sites of Struggle*, Case study of women workers in Noida, India.

[3] According to the Master Plan for Noida-2001.

[4] Surinder Jetley (1990): "Women in the Food Processing Industry" in Divya Pandey & Mira Savara (ed), 'Between the Farm and Thali-Women and Food Processing, Research Centre for Women Studies. S.N.D.T. Women's University, Bombay.

[5] Vijay, Rukmini Rao and Subha Hussain (1991): " Invisible Hand- The Women Behind India's Export Earnings" in Nirmala Banerjee (ed) *Indian Women in changing Industrial Scenario*, Sage Publications, New Delhi.

[6] Ashok Kundra (2000): *The Performance of India's Export Zones*, Sage Publications, New Delhi.p.29.

[7] Sharmila Peieis and Ranaraja, S. (2001): *Labour Issues in Export Processing Zones in South Asia*, I.L.O., New Delhi.p.328.

[8] Nirmala and Banerjee (1991): "The more it changes, the more it is the same-Women workers in Export Oriented Industries", in Nirmala Banerjee (ed), *Indian Women in a Changing Industrial Scenario*, Sage Publications, New Delhi.p.248.

[9] Beena (1991): "Technological changes and women workers: The case of Fish Processing Industry in Kerala", in Chetana Kalbagh (ed), *Women and Development*, Vol.1, Discovery Publishing House, New Delhi. P.216.

[10] Neera and Desai (1990A): "Women Food Processors- Work without Reward", in Divya Pandey & Mira Savara (ed), *Between the Farm and Thali-Women and Food Processing,* Research Centre for Women's Studies, S.N.D.T. Women's University, Bombay.p.86.

[11] Lalitha and Iyer (1990A): "Overview of Employment in the Food and Drink Industries" in Divya Pandey & Mira Savara (ed), *Between the Farm and Thali-Women and Food Processing,* Research Centre for Women's Studies, S.N.D.T. Women's University, Bombay.

[12] Beena (1991): "Technological changes and women workers: The case of Fish Processing Industry in Kerala", in Chetana Kalbagh (ed), Women and Development, Vol.1, Discovery Publishing House, New Delhi. P.216.

[13] Mathew (1991A): " Exploitation of Women Labour Employment in Kerala," in Chetan Kalbagh (ed), Women and Development, Vol. 2, Discovery Publishing House,New Delhi.p.184.

[14] Sharma and Sengupta (1984): "Women Employment at SEEPZ, Unit for Urban Studies, T.I.S.S. Bumbay. (Report prepared for Insian Council for Research on International Economic Relations. New Delhi). P.66.

[15] Vijay; Rukmini Rao and Subha Hussain (1991): " Invisible Hand- The Women Behind India's Export Earnings" in Nirmala Banerjee (ed) Indian Women in changing Industrial Scenario, Sage Publications, New Delhi.p.17.

CHAPTER-IV

CHAPTER - IV

EMPLOYMENT, HEALTH AND WORKING ENVIRONMENT OF WOMEN WORKERS IN THE VSEZ

4.1 Introduction:

In the preceding Chapter the socio-economic profile of the women workers in the VSEZ was examined. In this Chapter an attempt is made to analyse and examine the employment, health and working environmental conditions of the women workers in the VESZ. This Chapter is divided into two Sections. Section-I analyses the employment scenario of the women workers and health conditions that prevailed among the four units of the VSEZ. Section –II deals with the working environment and women problems in the VSEZ.

SECTION -I

In this Section employment and health conditions of women workers are examined in order to Study the problems and prospects of women workforce in SEZs in India and particularly in the VSEZ.

India's population grew from 236 million in 1891 to 1027 million in 2001. The net addition during 1991-2001 was 183 million as compared to that of 161 million during 1981-1991. However, average annual growth rate for all India has declined from 2.14 in 1980's to 1.93 in 1990's. The growth rate of employment declined sharply from 2.04 per cent per annum during 1993-94 to 1999-00. The task force on employment opportunities admitted deceleration in employment growth. "This sharp deceleration in the growth of employment has naturally been the focus of much attention and comment, raising fear that economic growth in 1990's has been of a 'Jobless' variety". (Planning Commission, 2001)[1]

4.1.1 Employment Opportunities in Other Countries:

The benefit of the employment generation on host economies has been highlighted by some studies. Though the number of jobs created in absolute terms is quite impressive, the impact on joblessness at the national level has not been significant. Employment generation is an important objective of EPZs in smaller countries. But in the case of large economies like India, EPZs have helped in generating additional employment, but their overall impact depends upon the size of the economy and stage of its development.[2]

In smaller economies, successful EPZs have a significant proportion of workforce in the manufacturing sector. This is true of EPZs in Mauritius, Mexico and the Dominican Republic. In Singapore, Malaysia and Srilanka, EPZ employment constitutes a high proportion of overall industrial employment, which ranges between 16 to 35 per cent. In Hong Kong, Mexico, Korea and Taiwan, it is estimated to be between five to six per cent[3]. EPZ employments are not substantial in India as their number is small and size is modest. However, Chinese zones have generated considerable employment in view of their large size and broader scope of permitted activities. A United Nations Industrial Development Organisation (UNIDO) study has estimated that employment in the Chinese zones in 1991 was as high as 2.2 million, out of worldwide EPZ employment of 4 million[4].

4.1.2 Employment Opportunities and Conditions in India:

In many countries, EPZs have generated a significant proportion of the industrial workforce. However this is not the case in India, where the EPZs share in organised manufacturing employment alone, would be less than one per cent. Overall employment in the zone has increased at an annual average of 17 per cent in the last decade, but this must be seen in conjunction with the disruption caused in individual or 'groups of workers' lives by the high rate of closures in the zones. Out of 789 units that became operational, 264 had ceased functioning by 1998.[5]

4.1.3 Women Workers in the SEZs:

A distinct feature of the SEZs is the high proportion of women in the workforce. Employers have a strong preference for women workers since it is believed that dexterity, patience and other "gender-specific attributes" make them more suitable than men for carrying out tasks that demand painstaking attention to detail and are repetitive. Women, regardless of their level of education, constitute the bulk of the unskilled and semi-skilled workers and this is particularly in the textile, clothing, leather and electronics industries. In India male workforce constitutes 57 per cent of the SEZs.

4.2 Employment in the VSEZ:

An Export-Processing Zone (EPZ) has been established in the year 1989 on the East Coast of India at Visakhapatnam city and has been named as Visakhapatnam Export Processing Zone (VEPZ) and 20 units were in operation. A few of these units are labour intensive, thereby generating employment opportunities to a considerable size, and has been one of the positive features of the VEPZ, now known as Visakhapatnam Special Economic Zone (VSEZ) since April 2001. The total employment of the zone at present is 2692 of which 1602 (59.51 per cent) are men and 1090 (40.49 per cent) are women (Table - 4.1). About 40 per cent of women workforce indicates that the employers of the units of VSEZ have a strong preference for women workers.

4.2.1 Year and Gender-Wise Distribution and Growth of employees in the VSEZ:

TABLE- 4.1

Year and Gender-Wise Distribution and Growth of Employees in the VSEZ

Year	Number of Employees			Gender-wise Growth Rates		
	Male	Female	Total	Male	Female	total
1996-97	10	0	10	-	-	-
1997-98	210	100	310	95.24	100.00	96.77
1998-99	236	113	349	11.02	11.50	11.17
1999-2k	1136	375	1511	79.23	69.87	76.90
2000-01	1196	387	1583	5.02	3.10	4.55
2001-02	1293	427	1720	7.50	9.37	7.97
2002-03	1326	916	2242	2.49	53.38	23.28
2003-04	1586	1087	2673	16.39	15.73	16.12
2004-05	1602	1090	2692	1.00	0.28	0.71

Source: Data collected from the office of the VSEZ, Visakhapatnam.

As shown ante italics.

The data of the Table 4.1 indicates that the total employment increased from 10 workers in 1996-97 to 2692 by 2004-05. Out of this males account for 59. 51 per cent (1602) and females account for 40.49 per cent (1090). The VSEZ is thus providing employment to women at the rate of about 40 per cent of its employees as evidenced by 100 women workers in 1997-98 that been increased to 1090 by 2004-05. Though 20 establishments are in operation in VSEZ the women employment is mainly concentrated in four establishments. The gender-wise distribution of employees of these four establishments is presented in Table 4.2.

4.2.2 Gender-Wise Distribution of workers in the VSEZ units:

TABLE 4.2

Gender-Wise Distribution of Employees in Selected Units of the VSEZ

Sl.No.	Units	Male	Female	Total
1	World Wide Diamond	628 (69.16)	280 (30.84)	908
2	Madras Knitwear Pvt. Ltd.	103 (31.40)	225 (68.60)	328
3	Bangalore Swatter Pvt. Ltd.	55 (36.67)	95 (63.33)	150
4	L.I.D.Jewellery Pvt. Ltd.	409 (50.25)	405 (49.75)	814
	Total	1195 (54.32)	1005 (45.68)	2200

The data of Table 4.2 indicates that the women workforce of the four units put together is accounting for about 45.68 per cent. Among these four units WWD and LID shows that the proportion of female workforce is less than the male workforce. Where as female workforce is higher in other two units i.e. MKW and BSW.

4.2.3 Working Experience of women in the VSEZ units:

TABLE- 4.3

Working Experience (in Years) of Women Workers in the VSEZ Units

S. No	Experience (in Years)	VSEZ Units					Per cent
		WWD	MKW	BSW	LID	Total	
1	< Two	12 (10.91)	21 (19.10)	16 (14.55)	61 (55.45)	110	35.38
2	Three – Four	56 (40.29)	26 (18.71)	25 (17.99)	32 (23.02)	139	44.69
3	Five – Six	35 (59.32)	05 (8.47)	09 (15.25)	10 (16.95)	59	18.97
4	> Seven	0	0	03 (100.00)	0	03	0.96
	Total	103	52	53	103	311	
	Per cent	33.12	16.72	17.04	33.12		100.00

Note: Figures in the parenthesis indicate percentages

Period of service is an important tool in measuring the workers hold on their employment. It indicates that the more the number of years of service, the more the security of employment. The distribution of workers according to their service with the present employers is presented in Table 4.3. A majority of the workers i.e., 44.69 per cent have put on three to four years of service with the present employers while 35.38 per cent have below two years of service and 18.97 per cent of workers have five to six years of service. Only a marginal per cartage (0.56) of workers are in the service for above seven years.

Among the four units of the VSEZ working experience of women below two years is highest in LID (55.45 per cent) followed by MKW (19.10 per cent), BSW (14.55 per cent) and WWD (10.91). Where as among women having three to four years and five to six years of experience is highest in WWD (40.29 and 59.32 per cent) followed by LID (23.02 per cent and 16.95 per cent). On the whole it may be inferred from the Table that the women workers gained better experience than other units in WWD. Even then, those who gained more experience still may not question the principal employer to provide better facilities because of the fear of insecurity of employment.

4.2.4 Training Period in the VSEZ units

TABLE-4.4
Training Period (in months) of Women Workers in the VSEZ Units

S. No	Training Period (in Months)	VSEZ Units					Per cent
		WWD	MKW	BSW	LID	Total	
1	Six	0	52	53	0	105	33.76
2	Twelve	103	0	0	103	206	66.24
	Total	103	52	53	103	311	
	Per cent	33.12	16.72	17.04	33.12		100.00

Note: Figures in the parenthesis indicate percentages

The women workers come from rural areas where life is slow with no pressure on time. The workers adjust remarkably well to the new environment but some problems remain, e.g. absenteeism, lack of commitment and low productivity. In order to enhance the skills and ability and to chose and shape their occupations, training is essential for the development of women. In order to examine the importance of training in the units of VSEZ, Table-4.4 shows the training period provided by different units for women respondents. It is observed from the Table that two units are giving six months training i.e., MKW and BSW, another two units are giving one year training i.e., WWD and LID. The proportion of the units giving six months training is nearly, 34 per cent and the proportion of the units giving twelve months training is 66 per cent.

4.2.5 Leave provisions in the VSEZ units:

TABLE-4.5
Leave Provisions of Women Workers in the VSEZ Units

S. No	Type of Leaves (in Days)	VSEZ Units			
		WWD	MKW	BSW	LID
1	Casual Leave	12	10	10	15
2	Earned Leave	15	12	15	15
3	Sick Leave	10	12	12	10
4	Maternity Leave	90 *	90 **	90 *	90 *

Note: * With 75 per cent salary ** with 50 per cent salary

The above Table shows that the leave provision for women workers in the units of VSEZ. The workers in these industries are eligible for twelve days of casual leave in some units. There are 10-15 days leave per year. And there is provision for earned leaves for 15 days in WWD, BSW, LID and 12 days in MKW per year. In VSEZ units, employees are eligible for 10-12 days of sick leave per year. There is provision for maternity leave for three months (90 days with 50 or 75 per cent of salary). Even Sundays are working days for them. The provision of leave is based on rotation. No possibility of availing public holidays. If the workers avail leave without prior permission, salary will be deducted.

Durganand Sinha did a study on 'job satisfaction in office and manual workers'. According to Sinha, job satisfaction is the complex of various attitudes possessed by an employee. These attitudes are related to the many aspects of the jobs such as wages, supervision, steadiness of employment, conditions of work, opportunities for advancement and such other specific factors. He concludes that the office group was more dissatisfied with their work. It also states that, salary and security may not appear important when workers are satisfied, but they come to the fore when they are dissatisfied[6]. A lot of work has been done on the theme of job satisfaction among industrial workers. Sophisticated techniques have been developed to measure its extent and also to identify various components of job satisfaction.

4.2.6 Job/work satisfaction in the VSEZ units:

TABLE-4.6
Job/Work Satisfaction of Women Workers in the VSEZ Units

S. No	Rate of Satisfaction	VSEZ Units					Per cent
		WWD	MKW	BSW	LID	Total	
1	Very much	30 (76.92)	02 (5.13)	01 (2.56)	06 (15.38)	39	12.54
2	Moderate	26 (38.81)	03 (4.48)	15 (22.39)	23 (34.33)	67	21.54
3	Like that	28 (31.82)	18 (20.45)	18 (20.45)	24 (27.27)	88	28.30
4	Not much	19 (16.24)	29 (24.79)	19 (16.24)	50 (42.74)	117	37.62
	Total	103	52	53	103	311	
	Per cent	33.12	16.72	17.04	33.12		100.00

Note: Figures in the parenthesis indicate percentages

Table 4.6 presents distribution of respondents in relation to job satisfaction. When respondents were asked whether they are satisfied with their present job there emerged four categories of respondents. It is evident from the Table that one third of the respondents showed satisfaction with their present job and out of this 12.54 per cent said that they like this work very much. About 37.62 per cent workers expressed they are not very much satisfied with the work. On the whole, it is important to note that two thirds of respondents are not satisfied with their job at all. Thus, the job satisfaction in the present Study is considered to be a product of satisfaction with one's skills, wages, satisfactory relations with supervisors and physical working conditions.

Desai's study of workers' expectations from supervisors and management reflects the role of supervisors between the workers and the management. The study highlights the following characteristics for a good supervisor, viz., to treat them as human beings, to help them in their work, be friendly, cooperative, impartial and not using much authority[7]. In another study concluded by John Zechariah, the workers expect he should use only minimum authority and restrain from being partial. The workers in his study also wished that they should not be exploitative since they are weak and poor. Therefore, the removal of incompetent supervisor is always necessary for the improvement of personal relations[8].

4.2.7 Working Relationships with Management in the VSEZ units:

TABLE-4.7

Working Relationships with Management of Women Workers in the VSEZ

S. No	Relationships	VSEZ Units					Per cent
		WWD	MKW	BSW	LID	Total	
1	Very Cordial	10 (16.95)	16 (27.12)	15 (25.42)	18 (30.51)	59	18.97
2	Cordial	18 (38.30)	08 (17.02)	09 (19.15)	12 (25.53)	47	15.11
3	Partly Cordial	25 (27.47)	20 (21.98)	19 (20.88)	27 (29.67)	91	29.26
4	Not Cordial	50 (43.86)	08 (7.02)	10 (8.77)	46 (40.35)	114	36.66
	Total	103	52	53	103	311	
	Per cent	33.12	16.72	17.04	33.12		100.00

Note: Figures in the parenthesis indicate percentages

Satisfaction regarding relations with management is presented in Table 4.7. These relations with management are reported to be discordial with respect to a majority of respondents nearly 65.92 per cent. Only 18.97 per cent are considered to be very cordial and 15.11 per cent have cordial relations with their management. Some of the women workers grieved about the misbehavior of the certain personnel in the management. There are even cases of sexual exploitation in night shifts by the managers. Even though they are doing their best, some supervisors insist the women workers to do the work speedily. In such cases also the workers considered them as not cordial.

4.3 Working Conditions in SEZ:

Employment generation is an important objective of SEZs in smaller countries, but may not be so in the case of large economies like India. SEZs help in generating additional employment, but their overall impact depends upon the size of the economy and the stage of its development. A unique feature of VSEZ employment structure is its feminisation due to the overwhelming presence of diamonds and knitwear units. In these units there is repetitive work, like assembling, which requires low-level skills for which women are popularly considered to be more eminently suited. It has been observed that employment of women workers is high in the Dimond units and knitwear units. The preponderance of young female workers in VSEZ has raised many social issues, which has been the subject matter of intense academic debate. These relate to their working conditions, wage rates and other fringe benefits. In VSEZ the wage rates for female workers are lower than male workers and the hours of work are longer than the norm in industrialised countries. However, studies have established that working hours in SEZs are not more than prevailing national average[9]. Wage rates in VSEZ are low in comparison with the international standards. Studies conducted by the International Labour Organisation (ILO) through the Asian Regional Team for Employment Promotion (ARTEP) during the eighties concluded that wage rates in Bataan and Masan (Indonesia) SEZs were lower than in the domestic tariff area. In Malaysian zones, they were at par with, and in Sri Lanka a little higher than, the wage rates in the domestic economy[10]. It can be safely presumed that wage rates in SEZs, more or less, approximate the respective national average.

Trade union rights in most of the SEZs are, however, somewhat curtailed. The Republic of Korea Prohibited labour disputes in the zones by a special enactment in 1970. In Singapore, the Industrial Relations Act of 1948 made dismissals non-negotiable. The same policy was applied in Malaysia in 1971. In the Philippines, strikes are expressly prohibited in 'vital' industries. In Sri Lanka, the entry of trade unions is barred in SEZs. In India, SEZ units have been granted public utility status under the Industrial Disputes Act 1947 by the respective state governments, prohibiting wildcat strikes without recourse to reconciliation proceedings. In VSEZ in the initial years after its establishment, a leader of Indian National Trade Union Congress (INTUC) led the functioning of union. However, the union did not work well. Later in 1988 the local workers formed a union and it is affiliated to a local chapter of Centre of Indian Trade Unions (CITU). But there is no improvement in the situation of the workers who are working in these units. In some units, there is no trade union activity.

4.4 Health Conditions of Women Workers in the SEZs:

Health is a state subject according to Article 47 of the Constitution of India. Accordingly, "the state shall regard the raising of the level of nutrition and the standard of lives of its people and the improvement of public health as among it primary activities and, in particular, the state shall endeavourer to bring about prohibition of the consumption of intoxicating drinks and of drugs which are injurious to health".

The joint ILO/WHO Committee on Occupational Health defined occupational health as "the promotion and maintenance of the highest degree of physical, mental and social well-being of workers in all occupations. the prevention of departures due to health caused by their working conditions, the protection of workers in their employment from risks resulting from factors adverse to health; the placing and maintenance of the work, in occupational environment equipment and to summarise: the adoption of work to man and of each man to his job".

The Committee recommended certain measures for women and children also. The protection of the health of pregnant women who are employed is of the first priority. All employed women should be placed in jobs, which are suitable to their physical abilities. Where women with young children are compelled to work, the provision of properly supervised day-care centers may be helpful. Young persons may be medically examined before their employment to determine whether they are fit to work or not. They should be placed only in jobs within their physical and mental capacities. They should also be periodically re-examined to assure that their health is not being adversely affected. Jobs.

which are hazardous, are prohibited for women and young persons in certain countries. Measures of health and labour protection are intended to enable the worker to obtain and retain suitable work and not to deny employment.

Mental health is as important as physical health. Psychoneurosis has been 'found to be a major cause of sickness absenteeism. The attitude of work supervisors will influence the mental health of workers working under them. Special attention should be paid in the selection of supervisors in order to maintain good human relation, which increases the effectiveness of health service activities, which is directly related to the health of the workers.

Dastur[11] as an industrial health consultant, made an earnest attempt to probe into the ideas, which are gathered during his lifetime in his book 'A Doctor's Approach to Industrial Medicine'. His view on industrial medicine is clear and authentic with a motive for welfare of the employee. He says, an industrial worker faces four kinds of hazards- physical, chemical, biological and psychological. Physical hazards arise from unguarded machines, dust, ventilation, illumination, wrong posture and so on; the use of poisonous chemicals leads to chemical hazards; handling of raw materials infected with germs causes diseases; whereas disregard to basic human needs like sense of security and belonging, status, recognition, self-importance, and so on is the cause for psychological hazards. These hazards can create medico-social problems for the individual, his family, his community and even to the industry itself. The way to control them is a many-pronged programme of an industrial health service consisting of preventive and constructive medical aid, environmental hygiene, mental hygiene welfare work and research.

The Report of World Health Organisation[12] states that social conditions like housing, crowding, nutrition, mode of transportation, necessity for extra earnings etc., are clearly related to the prevalence of various diseases, body weight, height and even life expectancy. In many regions ambient industrial air pollution is high, thus increasing the total exposure of the workers. There tend to be differences in exposure, even for workers performing the same work, owing to differences in patterns of movement, experience in handling the work task, personal cleanliness, etc. There may be a considerable range in personal exposure patterns of different employees. This applies not only to chemical exposure, but also to physical workload, heat, cold, noise exposure etc.

Veena Shatrugna[13] compiled data on 'Women and Health', which would be useful to women in the women's organisations, grassroots level workers and others concerned with those issues. The author pointed out the death of studies on the health problems of women. She says, this area is very crucial because women, who work long hours in the low paid unskilled jobs, are also the last to get organised. Hence, health problems related to the work place, hazards of pollutants on women working during childhood, adolescence, pregnancy and lactation could be dangerous to the women and the foetus. She concludes that there is very little information about the safe levels of these harmful substances and no amount of cash can compensate for the damage done.

Nirmala Banerjee[14] in her study on "The more it changes, the more it is the same Women Workers in Export Oriented Industries" commented women's occupations as low-paid, repetitive, require few skills and have little or no scope for advancement. It is a systematic attempt to study the status of working women in industries like frozen prawns, silk yarns, garments, leather goods, electric fans. The issues highlight how the vulnerable group of workers i.e., women, are being exploited in the capitalist mode of units and about the deteriorating status of women both at workplace and at home. The Study highlights those features which are specific to the Indian situation, in terms of sexual division of labour, and are very relevant to policy formulations, which in turn increases the status of working women both at home and at work-place.

Provision of health care facilities is necessary to ensure better health and improved productivity of labour. This is especially important for women who have less access to health care services. Government hospitals can be established near VSEZ. NGOs can provide certain types of health services and arrange for health insurance. The long experience of Gono Shahayyo Sangstha (GKS-Bangladesh), which combines provision of modern health care services with health insurance to ensure better facilities for people in programme areas, can be looked into. Women workers can also be provided with health education to teach about cleanliness, preventive health care, etc.

4.4.1 Awareness of Health Problems:

TABLE-4.8
Awareness of Health Problems Expressed by Women Workers in the VSEZ

S. No	Awareness about Health	VSEZ Units					Per cent
		WWD	MKW	BSW	LID	Total	
1	Yes	53 (28.04)	40 (21.16)	34 (17.99)	62 (32.80)	189	60.77
2	No	50 (40.98)	12 (9.84)	19 (15.57)	41 (33.61)	122	39.23
	Total	103	52	53	103	311	
	Per cent	33.12	16.72	17.04	33.12		100.0

Note: Figures in the parenthesis indicate percentages

Table 4.8 shows the awareness of the respondents towards their health problems particularly due to the working environment. Nearly 61 per cent of the total respondents are having awareness of health problems, but they are compelled to do long working hours and do not have strength to oppose the management. Among the total respondents 39 per cent of the women are unaware of the health problems. Ignorance of health problems may be due to lack of proper health education. It is the managements' responsibility to sensitise the workers towards the particular health problems related to their work, and make the workers to take necessary precautions.

4.4.2 Ailments / Diseases:

TABLE-4.9
Health Ailments / Diseases Affected to Women Workers in the VSEZ Units

S. No	Ailments / Diseases	VSEZ Units					Per cent
		WWD	MKW	BSW	LID	Total	
1	Dust Allergy	25 (40.32)	15 (24.19)	10 (16.13)	12 (19.35)	62	19.94
2	Eye Burnings	10 (21.28)	12 (25.53)	12 (25.53)	13 (27.66)	47	15.11
3	Headache	17 (35.42)	05 (10.42)	08 (16.67)	18 (37.50)	48	15.43
4	Body Pains	16 (32.65)	06 (12.24)	07 (14.29)	20 (40.82)	49	15.76
5	Irritations	15 (38.46)	08 (20.51)	04 (10.26)	12 (30.77)	39	12.54
6	Overheat	10 (40.00	0	0	15 (60.00)	25	8.04
7	Irregular Periods	10 (29.41)	06 (17.65)	09 (26.47)	09 (26.47)	34	10.93
8	Others	0	0	03 (42.86)	04 (57.14)	07	2.25
	Total	103	52	53	103	311	
	Per cent	33.12	16.72	17.04	33.12		100.00

Note: (The first complaint / opinion is taken into account for analysis)
Figures in the parenthesis indicate percentages

The women workers of the VSEZ units are a segment of the general population as the factor that influences the health of general population also applies to them equally, such as drinking water, sewerage, dust, waste disposal and nutrition. In addition, the health of these women workers, on a large measure, will also be affected by the conditions of their work place. Based on symptoms and prevalence of common diseases, health elements are identified among the women workers in VSEZ units. This study classified health elements into eight broad categories.

Ailments or diseases affecting the women workers in the VSEZ units are presented in Table-4.9. It is clear from the Table that on the whole, one fourth of the workers are affected by dust allergy followed by body pains, headache, eye-burnings, irritation and irregular periods to the percentage of 15.76, 15.43, 15.11, 12.54 and 10.93 respectively. Eight per cent of the workers are suffering with over heat. Among the different units of the VSEZ, employees suffering from dust allergy, irritations and irregular periods are highest in WWD. Whereas workers suffering from eye burnings, headache, body pains and overheat are highest in LID. It may be inferred from the Table that the larger proportions of the workers working in WWD and LID are affected by various health problems than the other two units, namely, MKW and BSW.

The respondents are facing with irregular menstrual problems due to mental stress associated with work environment, which has to be considered. An important aspect of individuals mutual health is the feeling of security or insecurity vis-à-vis her own well-being. The women engaged in insecure jobs are exposed to various forms of oppression and mental stress than those in secure jobs. The workers in these units usually work for eight hours or even more in standing position. Severe pain in legs, joints and muscles are common among these workers. Tasks like grading and packing require concentration and constant movement of body. Thus the nature of work is very tiresome and tedious.

4.4.3 Treatment Avenues:

TABLE-4.10
Treatment Avenues to Women Workers in the VSEZ Units

S. No	Treatment Avenues	VSEZ Units					Per cent
		WWD	MKW	BSW	LID	Total	
1	ESI Hospital	41 (32.03)	21 (16.41)	23 (17.97)	43 (33.59)	128	41.16
2	Private Hospital	25 (28.41)	13 (14.77)	17 (19.32)	33 (37.50)	88	28.30
3	King George Hospital	34 (40.48)	16 (19.05)	10 (11.90)	24 (28.57)	84	27.00
4	Others	03 (27.27)	02 (18.18)	03 (27.27)	03 (27.27)	11	3.54
	Total	103	52	53	103	311	
	Per cent	33.12	16.72	17.04	33.12		100.0

Note: (The first complaint / opinion is taken into account for analysis)
Figures in the parenthesis indicate percentages

Table 4.10 presents the treatment avenues by women workers in the VSEZ units. It may be observed from the Table that among total respondents, significant proportion (41.16 per cent) of the respondents working in various units of VSEZ are availing services provided by the ESI hospital. More or less equal proportion of respondents is utilising the services of private hospitals and King George Hospital. (28.30 per cent and 27 per cent respectively). Only 3.54 per cent of the respondents go to other treatment avenues due to availability of better facilities. Even though the VSEZ units have Employees' State Insurance (ESI) scheme a majority of the respondents are not utilising it due to the unsatisfactory services provided in ESI hospitals. Therefore, it may be suggested to establish super specialty hospitals in its own premises or it should reimburse medical expenses to its workers.

4.4.4 Reasons for not utilising ESI Hospital facility:

TABLE-4.11
Reasons for not Utilising ESI Hospital Facility by Women Workers in the VSEZ Units

S. No	Reasons for Not utilizing	VSEZ Units					Per cent
		WWD	MKW	BSW	LID	Total	
1	Poor facilities in ESI	25 (43.10)	08 (13.79)	11 (18.97)	14 (24.14)	58	18.65
2	No specialized Treatment in ESI	18 (24.32)	15 (20.27)	15 (20.27)	26 (35.14)	74	23.79
3	No facilities for serious conditions	50 (37.31)	20 (14.93)	19 (14.18)	45 (33.58)	134	43.09
4	Modern equipment in KGH/Private Hospitals	10 (22.22)	09 (20.00)	08 (17.78)	18 (40.00)	45	14.47
	Total	103	52	53	103	311	
	Per cent	33.12	16.72	17.04	33.12		100.00

Note: (The first complaint / opinion is taken into account for analysis)
Figures in the parenthesis indicate percentages

Table-4.11 shows that the reasons for not utilising ESI hospital facility by women workers in the VSEZ units. Out of the total respondents 43 per cent reported that ESI hospitals are not providing emergency services for serious conditions. Similarly, nearly 24 per cent of the respondents felt that there is no availability of specialised departments in the hospital. And more than 18 per cent of the total respondents reported that the facilities available in ESI hospitals are not satisfactory. The remaining respondents (14 per cent) felt that KGH is having better equipment and the specialists are providing good services in every department. Due to the above reasons most of the respondents are not utilising the services of the ESI and are getting treatment in the hospitals other than ESI.

4.4.5 Reasons for Utilising ESI Hospital Facility:

TABLE-4.12

Reasons for Utilizing ESI Hospital Facility by Women Workers in the VSEZ Units

S. No	Reasons for Utilizing	VSEZ Units					Per cent
		WWD	MKW	BSW	LID	Total	
1	Insurance Attachment	50 (37.04)	21 (15.56)	19 (14.07)	45 (33.33)	135	43.41
2	Nearness of ESI	25 (33.78)	10 (13.51)	14 (18.92)	25 (33.78)	74	23.79
3	Minor nature of Ailments / Diseases	16 (28.07)	14 (24.56)	12 (21.05)	15 (26.32)	57	18.33
4	Others	12 (26.67)	07 (15.56)	08 (17.78)	18 (40.00)	45	14.47
	Total	103	52	53	103	311	
	Per cent	33.12	16.72	17.04	33.12		100.0

Note: (The first complaint / opinion is taken into account for analysis)
Figures in the parenthesis indicate percentages

Table 4.12 presents the reasons for utilising the ESI hospital. About 41 per cent of the total respondents are utilising ESI hospital services. The reasons for utilising ESI hospitals are insurance attachment, nearness and convenience of taking treatment for minor ill health. About 43 per cent of the total respondents are taking treatment because of the insurance attachment. Nearly, 24 per cent of the respondents felt convenient to get treatment in ESI hospitals due to nearness. Out of the total respondents 18.33 per cent of the workers felt that facilities available in the ESI hospital are sufficient to treat minor illness or disease.

4.4.6 Suggestions to improve the quality of Employment Conditions & Environment:

TABLE- 4.13

Suggestions to Improve the Quality of Employment Conditions & Working Environment by Women Workers in the VSEZ Units

S. No	Suggestions	VSEZ Units					Per cent
		WWD	MKW	BSW	LID	Total	
1	Medical Facility with full salary	18 (32.14)	10 (17.86)	08 (14.29)	20 (35.71)	56	18.01
2	Maternity leave with full salary	15 (35.71)	09 (21.43)	06 (14.29)	12 (28.57)	42	13.50
3	Medical Checkup for every six months	10 (23.81)	07 (16.67)	07 (16.67)	18 (42.86)	42	13.50
4	Medical reimbursement for private treatment	15 (40.54)	05 (13.51)	04 (10.81)	13 (35.14)	37	11.90
5	50 percent reimbursement in emergency treatments	10 (33.33)	05 (16.67)	05 (16.67)	10 (33.33)	30	9.65
6	Crèche Facility	08 (40.00)	02 (10.00)	06 (30.00)	04 (20.00)	20	6.43
7	Company Hospital with Specialties	14 (34.15)	08 (19.51)	10 (24.39)	09 (21.95)	41	13.18
8	Company Bus facility	07 (22.58)	06 (19.35)	07 (22.58)	11 (35.48)	31	9.97
9	Uniformity in Salaries	06 (50.00)	0	0	06 (50.00)	12	3.86
	Total	103	52	53	103	311	
	Per cent	33.12	16.72	17.04	33.12		100.00

Note: (The first complaint / opinion is taken into account for analysis)
Figures in the parenthesis indicate percentages

The Table 4.13 gives the details of the suggestions given by the respondents to improve their quality of employment conditions and working environment. Majority of the respondents suggested that medical and maternity leave should be provided with full salary. And some of them expected to have free medical check-up in every six months. The respondents expressed to have a separate hospital on their own with all specialisations. Apart from this they expected to have reimbursement for private treatment, 50 per cent in case of emergencies, crèche facility, bus facility and uniformity in their salaries. Uniformity means equal payments for equal work to those who joined at the same time.

SECTION -II

In this Section an attempt is made to examine and analyse the working conditions of the women workers in India and particularly in the VSEZ.

4.5 Working Environment and Women Problems in the VSEZ:

Annabel Rodda's[15] book "Women and Environment" focuses on the importance of women in relation to environment and development. Her observations in the developing countries reveal that women's relationship with the environment is vital to their daily lives. The author mentioned about the women's role in food processing and described it as natural extension of women's work as food producers. These food-producing women who perform these tasks commercially will earn only a very low wage. Fish processing is a traditional activity of women in all coastal countries and fish are cleaned, processed and marketed by women only.

The occupational environment of the worker can be considered as a part of his domestic environment. Both are complementary to each other. Stress at work may disturb his sleep, just as stress at home may affect his work. According to ecological approach, occupational health represents a dynamic equilibrium or adjustment between the industrial worker and his occupational environment. The working environment is very important for both employee (for his health and welfare) and employer (for better production).

A distinctive feature of the VSEZ is the high proportion of women in the workforce. Employers have a strong preference for women workers since it is believed that dexterity, patience and other "gender-specific attributes" make them more suitable than men for carrying out tasks that demand painstaking attention to detail and are repetitive. Women, regardless of their level of education, constitute the bulk of the unskilled and semi-skilled workers and this is particularly pronounced in the diamond, garments, optical and other units.

4.5.1 Wages and Labour Standards:

There is an opinion that besides labour being cheap, wages in the developing countries are kept artificially low-by-low level of social protection. However, wage rates in the VSEZ units are low only in comparison with international standards. The ILO (1998a) notes that the minimum wage rates and take-home pay of workers in the VSEZ are higher than that of workers in similar factories outside. Even then they are lower than the revised minimum wage suggested by the Central Advisory Board in its meeting on 19-12-2003, and National minimum wage which has last been revised upwards to Rs. 66 per day with effect from 1-02-2004[16]. There is a contention that labour costs have to be kept low in order to attract investment. Labour costs and labour standards are a couple of factors that determine location of investment but are not crucial in them.

4.5.2 Labour Laws:

Certain governments have passed SEZ legislation that suspends the application of all or some labour laws in the zones. Workers may be prohibited from joining unions or engaging in any form of trade union activity. These prohibitions can be for an indefinite period. Bangladesh and Pakistan are good examples of countries where such measures have been taken. In India, SEZ units have been granted public utility status under the Industrial Disputes Act 1947 by the respective State governments, prohibiting wildcat strikes without recourse to reconciliation proceedings. In VSEZ in the initial years after its establishment the functioning of union was led by a leader of Indian National Trade Union Congress (INTUC). However, the union did not work well. Later in 1988 the local workers formed a union and it is affiliated to a local chapter of Centre of Indian Trade Unions (CITU). Even then there is no improvement in the situation of the workers who are working in these units. In some units, there is no trade union activity.

4.5.3 Training:

About 70 per cent of workers in the VSEZ are mostly rural, poor, young and unmarried women with little education. The women workers come from rural areas where life is slow with no pressure on time. The workers adjust remarkably well to the new environment but some problems remain, e.g. absenteeism, lack of commitment and low productivity. These problems can be ameliorated through basic literacy the curriculum should provide through understanding of the value of industrial discipline and globalised economy. The education and training programme should help women worker to acquire organisational skills.

4.5.4 Maternity Leave and Childcare:

Women workers are at a disadvantage when it comes to maternity leave. It is observed that the employers prefer young and unmarried women who have least family responsibilities and therefore can put long hours and uninterrupted work. But if the employment of married women is not discouraged, women would continue to work in the VSEZ. In this case, women should be allowed paid maternity leave for a certain period and employment security during pregnancy. A particular reason that discourages married women from continuing work in the VSEZ is the lack of childcare facilities, both at home and the work place. It has been suggested that childcare facilities should be provided in the VSEZ and working time of women should be adjusted to the timing of childcare centers.

4.5.5 Transport facilities:

Certain features of the labour market and labour, make arrangements for transport urgent. Predominance of women in the labour market, long distance from which they travel to work, night shifts and night travel make arrangements for transport necessary to ensure timely attendance at work. It is all the more necessary to ensure safe journey of women worker to and from work as miscreants on their way to and from work expose them to sexual attacks. It is heartening to note that units in VSEZ have made arrangements for the transport of workers.

4.5.6 Over-time allowance:

Section-59 of the Factories Act, 1948 provides for extra wages for overtime. If a worker works in a factory for more than nine hours in any day or for more than 48 hours in any week, he/she shall, in respect of overtime work, be entitled to wage at the rate of twice the ordinary rate of wages. In the VSEZ units over-time allowance earned by workers is very low. They are given overtime only when they work after the usual 10/12 hours of work. Most of them are young unmarried women from low socio-economic background; they usually do overtime to get the extra income.

4.5.7 Canteen Facilities:

In VSEZ there is no Canteen facility in some units. The workers are provided with tea allowance. There are no rest rooms for the women workers. In the lunch hour, the workers sit in the room filled with material, which is filled with dust. Except in some units there are no basic facilities. As per the provisions of Section 42 of the Factories Act, 1948, the workers are to be provided with running water, soaps and dettol to clean their hands and feet after finishing their work. But there are no such basic facilities in the VSEZ units.

4.5.8 Health care facilities and Health Insurance:

Provision for health care facilities is necessary to ensure better health and improved productivity of labour. This is especially important for women who have less access to health care services. Government hospitals can be established near the VSEZ. NGOs can provide certain types of health services and arrange for health insurance. The long experience of Gono Shahayyo Sangstha (GKS-Bangladesh), which combines provision of modern health care services with health insurance to ensure better of people in programme areas, can be looked into. Women workers can also be provided with health education to teach about cleanliness, preventive health care, etc.

4.5.9 Provident Fund:

In VSEZ though all the units are covered under the Provident Fund Scheme, a worker has to put up a minimum service of one year to get the provident found benefit. As such most of the workers are getting the benefit. Some workers are not willing to join in this scheme, because it is very difficult to collect the amount if they go to other units or other states. Among the women workers, only a few workers are getting the benefit of Provident Fund Scheme. The reasons are ignorance, unwillingness of the management to some extent, and unwillingness of workers to a major extent.

4.5.10 ESI Benefits:

Most of the units are covered under the Employee's State Insurance (ESI) Scheme. The units, which are outside the scheme reported that they have fewer workers than the minimum, required implementing ESI Scheme. Even the workers covered under the scheme are not satisfied with the facilities in the ESI Hospital in their region. There is no medical reimbursement provision in the VSEZ units. Most of the workers are spending from their pockets, when they fell sick. Some units are supplying first aid facilities. Workers suggested that they want company hospital and medical reimbursement provision in the emergencies.

4.5.11 Housing Services:

Women workers now live in private houses in groups or alone. There has been a growth in the supply of private housing services to meet the demand for such services by labour. However, it is not known whether the market for housing services is imperfect and workers are paying higher prices. If it is so, the situation can be improved by providing house, building loans to the private sector for constructing low-cost housing for labour. Government and NGOs can also make provisions for housing loans, which can be realised, from the workers over a period of time.

4.5.12 Public Utility Services:

In India, SEZ units have been granted public utility status under the Industrial Disputes Act 1947 by the respective state governments, prohibiting wildcat strikes without recourse to reconciliation proceedings[17]. As a result of these measures and insulation due to bonding, trade union activity in the zones is less intensive and incidence of disputes is much lower than in the domestic economy. In VSEZ, the State government may delegate the powers of the Labour Commissioner to the Development Commissioner of the VSEZ or to an officer of the state government who is posted exclusively. The supervisory bodies of the ILO use a very strict definition of the term public utility services: essential services are only those whose interruption would endanger the life, personal safety or health of the whole or part of the population. Though strikes and lockouts are low because of the public utility status, they are uncommon in the VSEZ in Visakhapatnam.

4.6 Conclusion:

In the VEPZ women constitute considerable proportion of the labour force. The nature of employment reveals the fact that except a few all the workers are temporary, which shows the insecurity of employment. The jobs they do are unskilled or low skilled. Men are given preference in the skilled and high profit jobs. At policy level, the importance of the distinct economic role of women in the zone is not reflected. On papers the national labour laws are applicable in the zone but in practice things are different. The working conditions and work environment show long hours of work, standing posture of work, lack of job security, lack of personal protective equipment, absence of labour unions, low wage rates and absence of non-wage benefits.

On women's health, the Study noted that the women, everywhere, are underdeveloped, work for long hours than men, undernourished and in poor health. The triple roles of being a home manager, economic provider and reproducer generate health problems and hazards in a number of categories, some derived from women's socio-cultural status, some from their reproductive role. These risks tend to reinforce each other to the detriment of their overall health status.

In VSEZ a majority of the women workers are unaware of health problems due to heavy work. Most of the workers bear their medical expenses on their own, due to the poor medical facilities provided by the units. Most of workers express severity in eye burnings and regarding the incidence of diseases like respiratory problems, skin diseases, lung infections, hyper acidity and body aches there is no health insurance scheme.

Jacobson[18] reported that globally, 66 per cent of all women live in poverty. Poverty and social status affect women's health. He stated more action is needed to improve women's health, otherwise the world will continue to lose more of women's prime. The global economic crisis had plummeted more and more households into poverty. Women place other needs above their own, resulting in poor health.

The women in VSEZ are largely anaemic. This is possibly because the diet they take lacks the nutrition their bodies need to cope up with the hard labour they put in during their day-long toil in the industry as well as at their homes. The knitwear units in the zone have seen strict time schedules. No special facilities are provided for women in the zone. A special doctor to look after the specific problems and diseases for women can be thought of even when there are normal minimal medical facilities, especially if the factory premises employ more than 30 women. However, such facilities were seldom seen even though most of the factory units in the zone employ more than 30 women. Health and safety is given the lowest priority not only by the management but also by the workers. The management feels that the production costs may go up by providing safe working environment, where as workers feel that issues like wage, bonus and job security are more important. "Daily bread for us and our family is more important even if it is at the cost of our health" is the general notion of a VSEZ worker.

Finally, the employment conditions, health and working environmental conditions of the VSEZ women workers are very poor and unhealthy.

CHART - 4.1 WORKING EXPERIENCE (IN YEARS) OF WOMEN WORKERS IN VSEZ UNITS

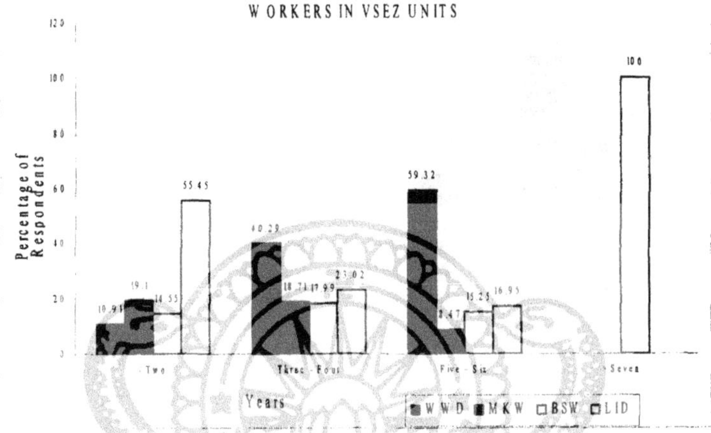

CHART 4.2 JOB SATISFACTION OF WOMEN WORKERS IN VSEZ UNITS

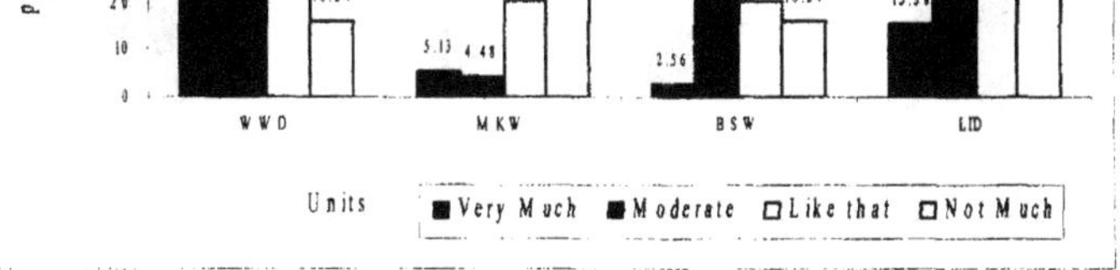

CHART 4.3 AWARENESS OF HEALTH PROBLEMS EXPRESSED BY WOMEN WORKERS IN THE VSEZ

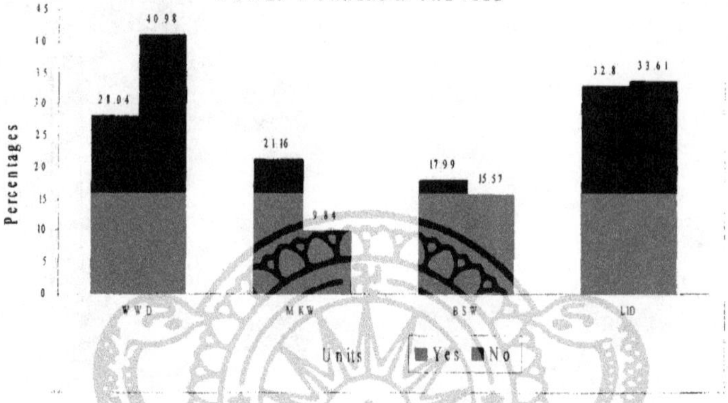

CHART 4.4 TREATMENT AVENUES TO WOMEN WORKERS IN VSEZ UNITS

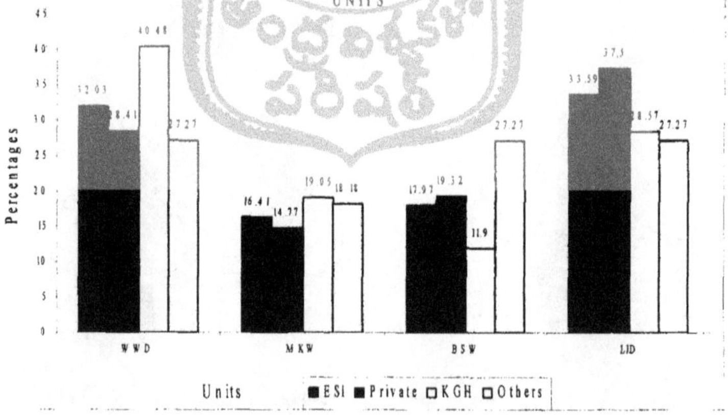

References:

[1] Government of India (2001): *Planning Commission Report*, Ministry of Finance.

[2] Madhavi, A.D. and Vijayalakshmi, M. (2001): "Freedom of Association and Promotion of Social Dialogue in EPZs of India", Ed in *Labour issues in Export Processing Zones in South Asia: Role of Social Dialogue* by A.S. Oberai, A. Sivananthiran and C.S. Venkata Ratnam, p.89.

[3] ILO/UNCTC (1988): *Economic and Social Effects of Multinational Enterprises in Export Processing Zones*, Geneva: ILO, 1988,p.20.

[4] UNIDO (1995): *Export Processing Zones: Principles and Practices*, Vienna, UNIDO, p.7.

[5] Indrani Majumdar (2001): "EPZs and their workers in India: A Study of the Noida Export Processing Zone" Ed in *Labour issues in Export Processing Zones in South Asia: Role of Social Dialogue* by A.S. Oberai, A. Sivananthiran and C.S. Venkata Ratnam, pp. 163-164.

4. Durganand Sinha (1998): "Job Satisfaction in Office and Manual Workers." *the Indian Journal of Social Work*, Vol.XIX, No. 1, June, pp 39-46.

[7] Desai, K.G. (1969): "A Study of Workers' Expectations from Supervisors and Management", *the Indian Journal of Social Work,* Vol. XXX, No.2, July, pp. 105- 115.

[8] John Zechariah (1983): "Employer's Expectation from a Supervisor", *The Indian Journal of Social Work,* XLIV, No.3, October, pp. 307-310.

[9] Lee and Eddy (ed) (1984): *Export Processing Zones and Industrial Employment in Asia*, Bangkok, ILO-ARTEP, p.6.

[10] Ibid. pp. 36-38.

[11] Dastur (1960): *A Doctor's Approach to Industrial Medicine*, Tata Institute of Social Sciences, Mumbai.

[12] World Health Organisation (1973): *Environmental and Health Monitoring in Occupational Health*, Geneva.

[13] Veena and Shatrugna (1994): "Women and Health", *The Indian Journal of Social Science*, Vol. 7, Nos. 3 &4, Sage Publication, New Delhi.

[14] Nirmala.B (1991): "The more it changes, The more it is the same-Women Workers in Export Oriented Industries", in Nirmala Benerjee (ed), *Indian Women in a Changing Industrial Scenario*, Sage Publications, New Delhi.

[15] Annabel and Rodda (1991): "Women and the Environment", Zed Books Ltd., London & New Jersey.

[16] J.Bhagya Lakshmi (2005): "Towards Equality at work" *Kurukshetra*, May, Vol. 53, No.9, p.23.

[17] Venkata Ratnam, C.S. (2001): *Labour Issues in Export Processing Zones in South Asia: Role of Social Dialogue*, South Asia Multidisciplinary Team (SAAT), New Delhi.p.91.

[18] Jocobson, J.L. (1993): "Women's Health: the price of poverty", in Koblinsky, M., Timyan, J. and Gay, J. (ed..), *The Health of Women: A Global Perspective*, Boulder Colorado, West View Press, pp.3-31.

CHAPTER V

CHAPTER -V

DETERMINANTS OF INCOME OF WOMEN WORKERS IN THE VSEZ

5.1 Introduction:

Employment, Health and Environment conditions of the women workers in the VSEZ were dealt in the previous Chapter. In this Chapter an attempt is made to identify the determinants of income of women workers in the VSEZ. The present Chapter is divided into three Sections. Section–I deals with the determinants of income. Section–II presents the case studies conducted during the period of Study along with data collection, and Section–III presents the levels of living of the women workers in the VSEZ.

Income, as the term is commonly used, is the money received in a given period of time by an individual as the earning from his property and from his productive services. In Economics, the term has a more specialised meaning, and applies not only to individuals or families, but also to other economic units, such as business firms or national economics.

The measurement of Income particularly for large economic units is a difficult task because of numerous complicating factors. For example, there is danger of duplication. The same income may be placed under two different readings and thus be counted twice. Also, prices change from time to time. As a result, the same amount of rupees may not command the same quantity of goods and services at two different times. The term real income is often used to describe income in terms of its purchasing power. The quantity of goods and services it will purchase.

SECTION–I

An attempt is made in this Section to examine the determinants of women's income in the VSEZ. The determinants of income assume importance, as there is need to increase incomes of women, which in turn enhance health, economic and social status of women.

Labour earnings, as observed earlier, have shown divergence across labour markets. Various explanations have been provided in the literature for such divergence. Mincer model of earnings based on the human capital approach has been widely used in the literature[1]. Earlier studies have widely adopted human capital based income earnings function to analyse the determinants and thereby heterogeneity, if any, in earnings in the labour market. As explained earlier, women in the urban informal sector witnessed variations in income earnings. It would be worthwhile to explore the causative factors and the present Study also makes use of the human capital studies; the present Study makes use of the human capital approach as the basis for analysing determinants of earnings. The results are analysed at aggregate and desegregate levels.

5.2 The Model

The basic model is generally specified as

$$Y = f(S, X, A)$$

Where

Y = earnings

S = schooling

X = length of experience, and

A = ability

Regarding the measurement of the variables, schooling is measured in terms of years of education; years of experience are taken to indicate length of experience while ability is measured by proxies for origin or family backgrounds[2]. However, this model is criticised on the following grounds. Firstly it may be difficult to correctly indicate schooling as a determinant of earnings. This could be so when schooling is measured in terms of years of education. Such measurement undermines quality aspect of schooling while taking care of quantity in terms of years of schooling. Students receiving same years of schooling may differ in their efficiency as firstly, given the same schooling receiving ability of students may differ and secondly, the quality of education offered across schools may vary. As such, students receiving same years of schooling may show different levels of efficiency. However, proxies for social background are expected to take care of this problem.

Secondly, this model assumes that higher the experience greater will be creation of human wealth. This positive association is assumed to be true based on learning by doing and on the job training. However, the quality of training offered and the possible divergence of its reception across labour would pose similar problem as that of the first criticism.

The third criticism is confined to the measurement of ability. The estimation of ability across workers poses similar problem. Certain personal attributes of workers may enhance their skill and thereby productivity. Moreover, migration[3], marital status and family size may be considered as important factors influencing the commitment of workers and thereby their earnings.

Lastly, this model is criticised for ignoring demand side aspects. As evidenced, labour market has a high probability of segmentation. This may be because "difference in earnings can be attributed to institutional factors after we have allowed for variations in measurable human capital factors"[4]. This may indicate that income variations apart, there may be a shift in the function itself depending upon the sectoral location of workers. This may also imply that segmentation gives rise to differential returns to the human capital variables leading to a change in the scope of earnings function for different sectors of the market." This may be the result of an invertible valuation in different sectors of the differential requirements of different activities in different sectors[5]". Despite the limitation "human capital model is quite robust in explaining individual variations in earnings[6]". Human capital model would thus be helpful after taking care of the limitations to explain differential earnings in the labour market.

The present Study makes use of the basic elements of the human capital model. It is modified to suit the needs of the Study. The basic form of the model is specified as:

Y= f (A, E, EXP, MS, SB,)

Where

Y = earnings of women workers

A = Age

E = Education

EXP = Experience

MS = Marital Status

SB = Social Background

5.2.1 Functional Form of the Model

Assuming that the variables bear additive influence linear form of the model is used in the present Study. Accordingly the model may be specified as:

Y=a + bA + cE + dEXP + eMS + fSB + U.

Where

Y= earnings of women workers

A= Age

E= Education

EXP= Experience

MS= Marital Status

SB= Social Background

b........f are the estimated parameters of the variables while U is the error term.

5.2.2 Measurement of the Variables

(a) **Age:** Age is measured in the conventional way assuming that higher the age higher the productivity and thereby earnings. Age is measured in number of years.

(b) **Education:** This is measured in terms of number of years of education completed as measured in the conventional way. Secondary education is represented as 10 years and the value 12 is given for those who have completed intermediate education. For those who have completed graduation the value of 15 is assigned to the variable. The variable takes the value of 17 if the women workers have completed post graduation.

(c) **Experience:** Experience is also measured in terms of years of work experience. The association is assumed to be positive as higher the experience higher will be the productivity and thereby earnings.

(d) **Marital Status:** If the women worker is married she may not necessarily work (in most of the cases) until she gets children because the income of the husband would be sufficient for the maintenance of the family. In that case the wife may take the role of only a housewife. It could also be true that wife may work in order to achieve a higher level of living. But in case of divorce, whose number is of a significant magnitude in the urban informal sector, they may be forced to work for their living. In such a case the relationship between marital status and earnings will be positive.

(e) **Social Background:** To capture the effect of quality differences in education and experience, marital status and social background dummies are used. The assumption is that more forward the caste of the worker, higher will be their quality, which positively influences earnings. The castes are grouped into three groups and accordingly three dummies are used.

D_1 = 1 if the women worker belongs to Forward Caste group 1 and '0' otherwise.

D_2 = 1 if the women worker belongs to Backward Caste group 1 and '0' otherwise.

D_3 = 1 if the women worker belongs to Scheduled Caste group 1 and '0' otherwise.

5.2.3 Results of the Regression Analysis:

The regression coefficients of the independent variable estimated through regression analyses together with their coefficients of multiple determinants ($\overline{R^2}$) are presented in this Chapter.

Table.5.1. presents the determinants of income in the WWD unit of the VSEZ. It can be seen from the Table that the estimated regression coefficients of independent variables like experience, age, married women and unmarried women are found to be statistically significant at 1 per cent level. The coefficient values of the independent variable EXP, A, MS d1 are 0.884, 0.468, 0.330 and 0.284 respectively.

It is clear from the Table that the estimated coefficient of variable EXP has the expected positive sign and it is significant at 1 per cent level in all income groups. This indicates its impact over the changes in the income. The estimated coefficient of variable A has the expected positive sign and it is significant at 1 per cent level in all income groups except in the group of less than Rs. 2000. This indicates its impact on all income groups except in the group less than Rs. 2000. Similarly the variables MS and E have shown their impact on income. The reason may be attributes to the increased employment opportunities and may not be that much of sensitive to the literacy level of the women workers in WWD unit.

The explanatory variables have explained 80 per cent of variation in case of total income of the sample respondents. The explanatory variables have explained 42 per cent of variation in case of income group of Rs.4001-5000, 35 per cent in case of income group of Rs.2001-

Table-5.1

Regression Coefficients of the Independent Variables at Different levels of Income – WWD unit.

Dependent Variable	Variables									Constant	$\bar{R}^2$	D.W
	A	E	MS	MS d_1	MS d_2	SB d_1	SB d_2	SB d_3	EXP			
Income	0.211 (1.924)	0.118 (0.256)	0.223 (1.209)	0.010 (1.000)	0.284 (0.445)	0.047 (0.015)	0.234 (0.024)	0.284 (0.421)	0.470* (7.786)	1361.386	0.148	1.728
Income	0.536* (3.009)	0.351 (0.401)	0.263 (1.890)	0.232 (1.574)	0.052 (0.679)	0.140 (0.023)	0.173 (0.037)	0.043 (0.659)	0.469* (12.174)	1130.925	0.355	1.158
Income	0.227* (3.572)	0.109 (0.476)	0.353** (2.244)	0.329 (1.868)	0.083 (0.827)	0.106 (0.027)	0.088 (0.044)	0.043 (0.782)	0.542* (14.451)	1897.388	0.319	0.906
Income	0.528* (3.271)	0.165 (0.436)	0.061** (2.055)	0.061 (1.711)	–	0.024 (0.025)	0.137 (0.040)	0.262 (0.716)	0.645* (13.234)	2844.361	0.422	1.473
Income	–	–	–	–	–	–	–	–	–	–	–	–
Total	0.468* (6.448)	0.082 (0.860)	0.330* (4.051)	0.284* (3.370)	0.138 (1.493)	0.005 (0.050)	0.008 (0.080)	0.131 (1.412)	0.884* (26.084)	710.290	0.804	1.538

Note: Figures in brackets indicate't' values

* Significant at the 1 per cent level.

**Significant at the 5 per cent level.

3000, 31 per cent in case of income group of Rs.3001-4000 and only 14 per cent in case of income group of less than Rs.2000.

The coefficients of the variable EXP at income level of less than Rs.2000 is found to be 0.470, followed by 2001-3000, 3001-4000 and 4001-5000 the values of which are 0.469, 0.542 and 0.645 respectively. The coefficient value of the variable A at income level of Rs.2001-3000 is found to be 0.536, followed by Rs.4001-5000 and Rs.3001- 4000 at values of 0.528 and 0.227 respectively. The coefficient values of the variable MS at income level Rs.3001- 4000 and Rs.4001- 5000 are 0.353 and 0.061 respectively.

Thus, in analysing the factors influencing the income of the women workers in the WWD unit, it is found that experience has the much influence on income than other factors. Variables like age and marital status shows some what less influence at various levels of income. Generally level of education influences the level of income but in case of WWD unit, it is not necessary to have higher levels of education as the nature of work does not require much technical know-how and so the levels of education does not show any impact on income.

Table.5.2. presents the determinants of income in the MKW unit of the VSEZ. It can be seen from the Table that the estimated regression coefficient of independent variables like experience, married women, age, unmarried women and women belonging to O.C. have found to be statistically significant at 1 per cent level. The coefficient values of the independent variable EXP, MS, A, MS d_1 and SB d_1 are 0.862, 0.424, 0.352, 0.346 and 0.257 respectively.

Table-5.2

Regression Coefficients of the Independent Variables at Different levels of Income – MKW unit.

Dependent Variable	Variables									Constant	$\overline{R^2}$	D.W
	A	E	MS	MS d_1	MS d_2	SB d_1	SB d_2	SB d_3	EXP			
Income	0.415** (2.051)	0.128 (0.206)	0.160** (2.620)	0.053** (2.006)	0.148 (0.978)	0.250 (1.398)	0.053 (0.897)	0.399 (0.541)	0.786* (10.883)	1102.931	0.551	0.817
Income	0.370 (1.802)	0.308 (0.181)	0.115** (2.303)	0.115 (1.764)	–	0.066 (1.229)	0.106 (0.789)	0.096 (0.476)	0.556* (9.567)	2472.019	0.332	0.889
Income	0.240 (0.874)	0.013 (0.087)	0.398 (1.117)	0.398 (0.855)	–	0.359 (0.596)	0.635 (0.382)	0.398 (0.230)	0.359* (4.640)	9037.500	0.456	2.156
Income	–	–	–	–	–	-	–	–	–	–		
Income	–	–	–	–	–	–	–	–	–	–		
Total	0.352* (3.092)	0.43 (0.310)	0.424* (3.950)	0.346* (3.025)	0.188 (1.475)	0.257** (2.108)	0.174 (1.353)	0.109 (0.816)	0.862* (16.407)	2003.899	0.759	1.378

Note: Figures in brackets indicate't' values

* Significant at the 1 per cent level.

** Significant at the 5 per cent level.

It is also clear from the Table that the estimated coefficient of Variable EXP has the expected positive sign and it is significant at 1 per cent level in income groups of less than Rs.2000, Rs.2001-3000 and Rs.3001-4000. It indicates that EXP has its impact over the changes in the income. However, in the other two income groups it is not significant. In case of married women, the estimated regression coefficient value has the positive sign and it is significant at 5 per cent level in income groups less than Rs.2000 and Rs.2001-3000. It is not significant in other income groups. In case of Variable A and MS d_1 they have positive sign and significant at 5 per cent level in the income groups of less than Rs.2000.

The explanatory variables have explained 75 per cent of variation in case of total income of the sample respondents irrespective of the income levels. Then explanatory variables have explained 55 per cent, 45 per cent and 33 per cent of variation in case of income groups less than Rs.2000, Rs.3001-4000 and Rs.2001-3000 respectively.

The coefficients of the variable EXP at income level of less than Rs. 2000 is found to be 0.786, followed by Rs.2001-3000 and Rs.3001-4000 the values are 0.556, and 0.359 respectively. The coefficients of the variable A at income level of less than Rs. 2000 are found to be 0.415, followed by Rs.4001-5000 and Rs.3001-4000 at values of 0.528 and 0.227 respectively. The coefficient values of the variable MS at income level of less than Rs.2000 and Rs.2001-3000 are 0.160 and 0.115 respectively. The coefficient value of the variable MS d_1 at income level of less than Rs.2000 is 0.053.

Thus, in analysing the factors influencing the income of the women workers in the MKW unit, it is found that experience has the much influence on income than other factors. Variables like age and marital status shows some what less influence at various levels of income. Generally level of education influences the level of income but in case of the MKW unit also it is not necessary to have higher levels of education as in the WWD unit, where as the levels of education does not show any impact on income.

Table.5.3. presents the determinants of income in the BSW unit of the VSEZ. It can be seen from the Table that the estimated regression coefficient of independent variables like experience (EXP), married women (MS), age (A), unmarried women (MS d_1), education (E), women belong to O.C. (SB d_1) and women belong to B.C. (SB d_2) have found to be statistically significant at 1 per cent level. The MS d_2 has a positive sign and significant at 5 per cent level. The coefficient values of these independent variables EXP, A, MS, MS d_1, E, SB d_1 and SB d_2 are 0.920, 0.770, 0.613, 0.448, 0.334, 0.304 and 0.266 respectively.

It is also clear from the Table that the estimated coefficient of variable A has the expected positive sign and it is significant at 1 per cent level in income groups of less than Rs.2000, Rs.2001-3000 and Rs.3001-4000. It indicates the impact of age over the changes in the income. However, in other income groups it does not have any impact of age on changes in income. In case of EXP the estimated regression coefficient value has the positive sign and it is significant at 1 per cent level in income groups of Rs.2001-3000 and Rs.3001-4000. It indicates impact of experience on income changes. As it does not found to be significant in other income groups it does not have any impact over the

Table-5.3

Regression Coefficients of the Independent Variables at Different levels of Income – BSW unit.

Dependent Variable	Variables									Constant	$\overline{R^2}$	D.W
	A	E	MS	MS d_1	MS d_2	SB d_1	SB d_2	SB d_3	EXP			
Income	0.444* (6.619)	0.612 (1.687)	–	0.524** (2.486)	0.524 (1.466)	0.078 (1.502)	0.226 (1.895)	0.242 (0.372)	0.935	1203.922	0.831	2.042
Income	0.043* (5.788)	0.121 (1.475)	0.238* (3.552)	0.238** (2.174)	–	0.242 (1.131)	0.429 (1.657)	0.242 (0.372)	0.110* (11.727)	2328.297	0.258	0.672
Income	0.510* (5.788)	0.094 (1.475)	0.077* (3.552)	0.077** (2.174)	–	0.047 (1.313)	0.144 (1.657)	0.188 (0.372)	0.586* (11.727)	160.694	0.623	1.664
Income	1.000 (1.000)	1.000 (1.000)	–	–	–	–	–	–	1.000 (1.000)	1500.000	1.000	–
Income	1.000 (1.00)	1.000 (1.000)	–	–	–	1.000 (1.000)	–	1.000 (1.000)	1.000 (1.000)	3400.000	–	–
Total	0.770* (11.466)	0.334* (2.922)	0.613* (7.037)	0.448* (4.306)	0.298* * (2.539)	0.304* (2.602)	0.266* (3.282)	0.098 (0.736)	0.920* (23.228)	143.608	0.839	1.804

Note: Figures in brackets indicate't' values

* Significant at the 1 per cent level.

** Significant at the 5 per cent level.

changes in income. In case of MS it has a positive sign and significant at 1 per cent level in the income groups of Rs.2001-3000 and Rs.3001-4000. Marital status of women workers shows some what less impact over changes in income. In case of variable MS d_1 they have a positive sign and significant at 5 per cent level in the income groups of less than Rs.2000, Rs.2001-3000 and Rs.3001-4000.

The explanatory variables have explained 83 per cent of variation in case of total income of the sample respondents irrespective of the income levels. Then explanatory variables have explained 83 per cent, 62 per cent and 26 per cent of variation in case of income groups of less than Rs.2000, Rs.3001-4000 and Rs.2001-3000 respectively.

The coefficients of the variable A at income level of less than Rs.2000 is found to be 0.444, followed by Rs.2001-3000 and Rs.3001-4000 the values of which are 0.043, and 0.510 respectively. The coefficient values of the variable EXP at income level Rs.2001-3000 and Rs.3001-4000 are 0.110 and 0.586 respectively. The coefficient values of the variable MS at income level of Rs.2001-3000 and Rs.3001-4000 are 0.238 and 0.077 respectively. The coefficient value of the variable MS d_1 at income level of less than Rs.2000 is 0.524 and in the income groups of Rs.2001-3000 and Rs.3001-4000 the values are 0.238 and 0.077 respectively.

Thus, in analysing the factors influencing the income of the women workers in the BSW unit, it is found that age, experience and marital status of women workers have to be found as influencing factors over changes in income. As in case of the WWD and the MKW units of the VSEZ education does not found to be influencing factor and do not place any impact over changes in income.

Table.5.4. presents the determinants of income in the LID unit of the VSEZ. It can be seen from the Table that the estimated regression coefficient of independent variables like experience (EXP), age (A), Education (E), married women (MS), unmarried women (MS d_1) and divorcee (MS d_2) have found to be statistically significant at 1 per cent level. The women belong to B.C. (SB d_2) have positive sign and significant at 5 per cent level. The coefficient values of these independent variables EXP, A, E, MS, MS d_1, MS d_2 and SB d_2 are 0.951, 0.590, 0.397, 0.245, 0.335, 0.258 and 0.186 respectively.

It is also clear from the Table that the estimated coefficient of variable EXP has the expected positive sign and it is significant at 1 per cent level in all income groups. It indicates its impact over the changes in income. In case of A the estimated regression coefficient value has the positive sign and it is significant at 1 per cent level in income groups of less than Rs.2000, Rs.2001-3000 and Rs.3001-4000. It is found to be an influencing factor only under the income groups of less than Rs.2000, Rs.2001-3000 and Rs.3001-4000. In case of E, the estimated regression coefficient value has the positive sign and it is significant at 1 per cent level in income groups of less than Rs.2000 and Rs.2001-3000. In case of MS it has a positive sign and significant at 5 per cent level in the income group of Rs.2001-3000. In case of variable MS d_1 they have positive sign and significant at 1 per cent level in the income groups of less than Rs.2000, Rs.2001-3000. In case of variable MS d_2, it has a positive sign and significant at 5 per cent level in the income group of Rs.2001-3000.

Table-5.4

Regression Coefficients of the Independent Variables at Different levels of Income – LID unit.

Dependent Variable	Variables									Constant	$\overline{R^2}$	D.W
	A	E	MS	MS d_1	MS d_2	SB d_1	SB d_2	SB d_3	EXP			
Income	0.070* (6.316)	0.483* (3.504)	0.244 (1.933)	0.244* (2.816)	—	0.157 (1.147)	0.154 (1.413)	0.014 (0.579)	0.434* (29.453)	785.990	0.273	0.601
Income	0.373* (6.316)	0.053* (3.504)	0.245** (1.933)	0.254* (2.816)	0.036** (2.053)	0.197 (1.147)	0.106 (1.413)	0.167 (0.579)	0.744* (29.453)	2553.318	0.537	0.901
Income	0.707* (3.447)	0.144 (1.912)	0.385 (1.055)	0.434 (1.537)	0.142 (1.120)	0.184 (0.626)	0.127 (0.771)	0.055 (0.316)	0.828* (16.074)	2287.188	0.803	2.123
Income	0.189 (1.303)	0.816 (0.723)	0.577 (0.398)	–	0.577 (0.423)	0.577 (0.236)	0.577 (0.291)	–	1.000* (6.075)	6300.000	1.000	–
Income	–	–	–	–	–	–	–	–	–	–		
Total	0.590* (9.260)	0.397* (5.137)	0.245* (2.833)	0.335* (4.128)	0.258* (3.010)	0.154 (1.682)	0.186** (2.071)	0.081 (0.849)	0.951* (43.176)	1109.578	0.914	1.638

Note: Figures in brackets indicate't' values

* Significant at the 1 per cent level.

** Significant at the 5 per cent level.

The explanatory variables have explained 91 per cent of variation in case of total income of the sample respondents irrespective of the income levels. Then explanatory variables have explained 100 per cent, 80 per cent, 53 per cent and 27 per cent of variation in case of income groups of Rs.4001-5000, Rs.3001-4000, Rs.2001-3000 and less than Rs.2000 respectively.

The coefficients of the variable A at income level of Rs.3001-4000 is found to be 0.707, followed by Rs.2001-3000, Rs.4001-5000 and less than Rs.2000 the values are 0.373, 0.189 and 0.070 respectively. The coefficient values of the variable EXP at income level of Rs.4001-5000, Rs.3001-4000, Rs.2001-3000 and less than Rs.2000 are 1.000, 0.828, 0.744, and 0.434 respectively. The coefficient values of the variable E at income levels less than Rs.2000 and Rs.2001-3000 are 0.483 and 0.053. The coefficient values of the variable MS at income level of Rs.2001-3000 is 0.245. The coefficient values of the variable MS d_1 at income level of less than Rs.2000 and 2001-3000 are 0.244 and 0.254 respectively.

Thus, in analysing the factors influencing the income of the women workers in the LID unit, it is found that experience, age, education, married women, unmarried women and divorcees are found to be influencing factors over changes in income. As expected, education found to be an influencing factor over changes in income, which is not so in other selected units of the VSEZ.

On the whole, the only influencing factor found to bring changes in income in all four units is experience. It is found that, except in case of the LID unit, education has no influence over changes in income of the women workers of the selected units of the VSEZ.

SECTION -II

5.3 CASE STUDIES

In any case it could be observed that the variable under the human capital model only explains a lower percentage of variation in income. This indicates that there is imperative need to explore other possible explanatory factors. Case Study method is resorted to explore this possibility. Ten case studies are presented hereunder.

5.3.1 Case Study: No- 1 (WWD Unit):

NagaLakskmi, a young girl of 21 years is working in the WWD Unit for the last two years. She is the only daughter of tailoring parents. She is having a brother who is 19 years old, and who is still studying. Every member of the family involves in tailoring, as it is a semi-skilled occupation, more so when it is home-based. At present, NagaLkshmi's mother helps her husband in tailoring besides household activities.

Two years back (2002) after completion of ITI (Industrial Training Institute) course, Nagalakshmi had joined the WWD Unit of the VSEZ through a paper notification and a formal interview. She is earning Rs. 2,500/- per month. The difference between the formal and informal sector is very categorical in the incomes of Nagalakshmi and her father, the former in formal sector while the latter in informal sector, but their incomes are equal now. Nagalakshmi's father's experience of nearly twenty years in tailoring did not fetch him any increments, where as his daughter could achieve it. This is the power of education (training in skills) and organised sector. Nagalakshmi's mother who attends to household and tailoring activities likes her daughter to stay at home and look after the household chores as well as tailoring, as she often spends leisure time with her friends, which normally a mother dislikes, but an adolescent girl, that too an earning girl likes to enjoy the company of girls of her age group. Poor mother often complains of Nagalakshmi's irresponsible behavior to her father, but in vein. Such repeated complaints at family level ultimately forced Nagalakshmi to take up tailoring activity, whenever there is a leisure time, rather than disappoint her mother. She lends money from her earnings to her mother only when there is any urgency.

They were in Vizianagaram and as tailoring does not provide sufficient income to run the family, her father influenced by relatives, brought his family to Visakhapatnam city. In this city her father earns more money and is satisfied with other income. Nagalakshmi completed I.T.I. She faces few problems with regard to family burdens, because only she likes to migrate. She joined WWD in 2003 through paper notification. She feels satisfied with this job. At the same time she is also facing some problems. They are lack of company bus facility, lack of other facilities like crèche to workingwomen etc. Yearly once, they go to their native place, and they send Rs.1000/- per month to her grandfather and grandmother for their maintenance. They don't want to get domestic commodities from their native place. This is a case of an unmarried girl who spends lavishly and she enjoys work and good food. This adolescent girl loves to mingle with different types of people and shares her joys with others.

5.3.2 Case Study No- 2 (WWD Unit):

Haritha is a migrant worker aged 23 years. She belongs to the agricultural caste of Kapu. She is working since the last 5 years. She hails from the village of Powerpet in Eluru in West Godavari District. Her father migrated to Visakhapatnam city in the year 1999 for taking up a job. Earlier, her father was doing a private job in their native place. It is not sufficient to run their family. He shifted to Visakhapatnam to seek a job that can provide sufficient income to run the family. Their relatives, who also supported him during the six months he took to get the job, persuaded him. Haritha completed X class only. Because of their family's expenditure she joined the VSEZ in WWD unit as a worker. She is doing the job for the last 5 years. The company pays Rs. 4,000/- per month as salary. She uses Rs.350/- for bus pass out of her earning. She gives the remaining amount to her father. Her father maintains the family. She reads books and sings religious songs on holidays or spends her leisure time with other workers who gather around her to listen to the religious songs.

Haritha hopes to raise her self to a better position in the company. She received training from company for one year. She recommends it for all the workers in the training period. She puts in hard work for 9 hours in a day. The reasons behind her entering this company were purely economic. She is independent earner now. In a week, she works over-time for 15 hours. She obtains Rs.300 (15x20) extra money along with her salary. Now she is satisfied with her job. She supports her family with this income. She suggested to the company about the improvements to be done in the conditions of work and for the workers. She said that rate of payment should be increased for women workers, and they should take better care of the health status of their women workers. The rate of incentives and over-time rates should also be increased to improve the working conditions. Then workers would feel economic security and they will show more interest in increasing the productivity of the company.

5.3.3 Case Study No- 3 (LID Unit):

Vijaya Vani is a 29-year old lady, who along with her family members lives in a mixed type of house. She originally hails from Challapalli near Vijayawada in Krishna District. Besides her, her father, mother and sister stay with her in the house. They are almost illiterate. The main source of income is business. The family earns Rs. 9000/- per month. The reason behind entering this unit was economic. She is independent earner now. Usually she works during night shifts. In a day, she works for 8 to 12 hours. The reason is partly due to lower social status of her family. She obtains a salary or Rs.4,000 per month from this unit including over-time and other incentives. She completed X class. She received training from the company for one year. She recommends this work for her friends also. She is independent earner now and is also satisfied with the job. She supports her family economically through this job. That's why they live happily. Her sister also gets a salary Rs. 1,500/- and she also supports her father financially. This is a case of an unmarried girl who has migrated to the city from a village. However, she said that the rate of payment should be increased and working conditions should be bettered. She also suggests that the women workers need the company bus facility, sanitary facilities and crèche facilities. If company bears the medical expenditure in the emergencies, the workers will feel secure. To improve the medical conditions, the company should direct private hospitals and not just

E.S.I. and K.G.H. in emergences. It would provide health security to the employees.

5.3.4 Case Study No- 4 (LID Unit):

Sunitha is a 28 year old married woman. She lives in a rented house near the VSEZ. Theirs is a small family. She stays with her husband and son, who is just 2 years old. Her Husband is a businessman who earns Rs. 5000/- per month. Business is not the traditional occupation for the family. It has been a practice adopted during 1998 by Sunitha in order to assist the family economically. In this way, monthly income of the family has grown to 7500/-. Originally the family is from Madhya Pradesh. She is attached to the VSEZ since 1999. She is the first in the family to join this work. She entered in this job for earning and supporting her family. She works for 10 hours in a day. She received one-year training from the company. She has been training all the trainee workers since 2000.

Social status of the VSEZ workers is not good. She suggests increase in the wages to improve the economic status of the women workers of the VSEZ. She feels that the working environment and other non-wage benefits should also be increased to suit the I.L.O. rules. They enjoy their jobs and then their socio-economic conditions have also improved. Sunitha has a suggestion to improve the working condition of the VSEZ women workers. Some times she feels insecure during the night shifts. So, she suggests that night duties should be allotted only after finding the willingness of workers. She likes to do only general shift duty because of her baby son. She says that night shift duty is inconvenient to her though she likes night duties. She suggests that the rate of wages must be increased, and maternity leave must be sanctioned with full salary and not just 75 per cent of the salary. These are the main suggestions from Sunitha. This is a case of a married woman who has migrated to the city coming out of the traditional system.

5.3.5 Case Study No- 5 (LID Unit):

Hemalatha is a 30 year old married Christian woman. She lives in a kaccha rented house. The family of four includes her husband and two daughters. Her children are in the age group of 18-14 years. All are literates and received primary education. Her husband is a small businessman, who earns only Rs.1,500/- per month as salary. She joined in this unit during the year 2001 in order to assist family financially. Her family friend encouraged her to take up this job. Now she is working independently. Usually she works during night shift in all the seasons. Because during the daytime, she does her family work and takes care of the children. Usually she works 8 to 13 hours in a day. She gets a salary of Rs.3,800/- per month. This is more than her husband's salary in the family. She herself manages the total family affairs. Before taking up the job, she was just a housewife. She is motivated by her family friend to enter this job. Now she is independent and feels economically secure because of this opportunity. She feels that rules and regulations should make the employees comfortable. She suggests increase in over-time wages and housing allowances. Or else housing facilities should be provided, she says. She also suggests that implementation of I.L.O. rules to provide total benefits. She suggests if medical facility and proper housing were provided near their unit, the working capacity and interest of the workers would increase.

She is also facing harassment due to caste feelings in the unit. She belongs to a backward class. Another important suggestion from her is equal salary for equal work for employees who joined together. She visits her native place Korukonda, near Rajahmundry in East Godavari District once in three months. She sends Rs.200 to her mother-in-law for pocket money every month. Hemalatha is so experienced in her work that she is paid Rs.20 per hour for over-time duty. She is well acquainted with the advantages of earning money and benefits. She suggests that wage rates and working conditions must improve for the women workers in the unit. She not only reflects the values and norms of her community but also adopted values and lifestyle that are totally alien to rural life. She hopes that she will continue as a worker till her daughters are married. This is a case of a married woman from a backward class who has migrated to the city and came out of extreme poverty.

5.3.6 Case Study No- 6 (MKW Unit):

Annapurna is a married woman worker of 29 years age. She entered this unit when she was 26 years. She dwells in a colony close to the VSEZ with lives with her husband. She belongs to backward class community. For the last three years, she has been working as a diamond polisher. At the end of the month she earns Rs.2,800, including over-time wages and incentives. Whatever is earned is given to her husband to maintain the family. She is not happy with this job because the wages and incentives are very low, and over-time payments meager. She took up this job to assist her family economically. Her neighbour persuaded her to enter this unit for job. She is working independently now. Usually she works during night shifts and afternoon shifts in all the seasons. She works for about 8 to 11 hours a day. After finishing her daily chores, she goes to the job comfortably. Now almost three years have passed but Annapurna economic status has not changed and still she remains poor. The money she had saved is with the bank but it's only a small amount. She feels that she must save something for herself and for her family for the future. Her family income per month is around Rs.4,600. She spends Rs.1,500 on non-food items and Rs.2,000 on food. She also manages to send money to her mother-in-law's family. This is the reason for Annapurna's entry into this job. She hopes that some day she will be able to fulfill the needs of her family. Her husband is a tailor and earns Rs.1,800 per month. It is less than Annapurna's income. She suggests that if the company pays traveling allowances, a part of her salary can be used for other economic activities. She likes equal payment for equal work for employees with same experience, and also wishes that the company takes care of the medical expenses and conducts medical check-ups for the women workers in the industry. If work environment improves, it provides job satisfaction and she feels the quality of work and productivity too will improve.

5.3.7 Case Study No- 7 (MKW Unit):

Madhuri is 22 years old. She has been working for the last two years in the Madras Knitwear unit. Her family consists of her father, mother and her only daughter. She feels that her father's income or Rs.2,000 per month is very less and not enough to maintain a family in the city. This forced her to take up this job to supplement to the family income. Her uncle supported her in getting this job through paper notification. She helps her father in earning that extra income. She completed a diploma course in education. She is a permanent resident of Vijayawada city in Krishna District. She is the first lady in the family who, due to economic reasons, took up employment during the year 2003. Her neighbour Praia, seeing her condition encouraged her to join this unit. Usually she works in the 8.30 a.m. to 5.30 p.m. general shift. Some times she has to work over time and gets OT. She has to work for 9 to 12 hours in a day. She received training from the company for a year.

She earns Rs.1,800 per month as salary from this unit. This is including incentives and over-time wages. She suggests that social status and income levels of these unit workers are not up to the mark. They face medical problems because of dust from the wool in this unit. Because of dust particles, they face dust irritation, and irregular periods and also get lung infections. So she suggests improvement in working conditions and salaries, and says non-wage benefits are a must and should be implemented to improve the productivity of the workers. She suffers with low wages, high or heavy working hours, less payments for over-time work and it affects her mental condition. So, she thinks that the government should take care about the working conditions in these units. The company must get involve to solve the problems of the workers. She suggests that the company must provide traveling facilities or a bus pass to the employees. Most of the time is wasted waiting for bus, as there is no bus facility provided by the company. She feels tensed about the work and is afraid of getting late to work as she depends on public transport. This is a case of an unmarried girl, who has migrated to the city and has come out of tradition lifestyle.

5.3.8 Case Study No- 8 (BSW Unit):

Bhanumathi is 31 years old and a married woman. She has been working in this unit for the last three years. Her family consists of two children and her husband. Her daughter earns Rs.1,000 per month. Her husband is a small business man and earns Rs.3,500 per month. Her son is studying for a degree. Her family expenditure is more than her husband's income and that is the reason for her to take up this job. After marriage, a family friend Ramesh, who is also doing business in this city, persuaded her to join this job. Earlier, after coming to this city she was living as a housewife. Then to support her husband's income to meet the household expenditure, she sought this job. She also heeded to the suggestion of her neighbour who advocated her to take up a job to earn the extra income. Both she and her daughter carry out the morning household chores before going to work. She lives in a rented house in a colony near the workplace. She belongs to OC category and hails from a forward social community. She converted into Christian religion. Bhanumathi took up this job to assist her family economically and socially. She received training from the unit for six months. The reason behind entering in this job was purely for economic reasons. She loves to mingle with different types of people and shares her joys with others. She is a member in C.I.T.U., a labour union. She puts in hard work for 9 to 12 hours in a day.

She was not very happy with her job conditions, as she has to stand during the working hours, which lead over heating of the body and other health disorders. She said that the rate of payment should increase and the workers must fight for their rights. She is unable to provide suggestions for improvement in the conditions of work. The company should safeguard the employees during the working time, and she also wishes a rise in the over-time wages and improvement in other infrastructural facilities like sanitation, medical allowances, and also crèche facilities in the unit. Full salary should be paid for maternity leaves, she feels. This will provide job security for the newly married girls in the unit. This is the case of married women worker in the VSEZ.

5.3.9 Case Study No- 9 (BSW Unit):

Harathi is an 18 year old girl. Her parents are doing a private job. Like the other young girls, Harathi loves to dress and enjoy life. She finished her Intermediate and studied civics, economics and commerce as her subjects. Her daily duty is to assist her mother in the household chores. By 7.00 a.m. she is ready to leave for work. She loves traveling, at times Haritha along with her group of women friends travel to distant places like Anakapalli, Bhimili etc in the holidays. She likes to eat good food and spends more time to prepare fast foods. After finishing Intermediate education, she did not like to waste time on further studies because of the economic status of her father. If she continues to study, her father will worry about her marriage and the fear of dowry haunts him. That's why she did not continue her education and thinks to support her father economically. On the advice of her friend Sowmya she joined in this job after the paper notification. For the past one year she is doing this job as a trainee in the Bangalore Swatters unit. She earns Rs.1,500 per month. In this way the monthly income of family has gone up to Rs.4,500/-. Originally the family is from Srikakulam. She entered in this unit for earning and supporting her father economically and to improve their social status. Out of their total family income that is around Rs.4,500 they spend Rs.2,500 on food and Rs.1,500 on other non-food items. Even after all these expenses, they save Rs.500 per month and invest in postal savings. It is a very poor saving but they cannot save anything more.

She suggests that the company must increase the salaries, over-time allowances and non-wage benefits. She feels a change in the working hours and working conditions will increase their productive capacity and job satisfaction. She also suggests that implementation of I.L.O. rules towards workers. The company must protect special benefits to the women workers regarding medical emergencies. She likes reasonable wages from the company. She prefers an independent life, enjoys and dreams of good things in life. This is the study of an adolescent girl.

5.3.10 Case Study No- 10 (BSW Unit):

Devichaitnaya is 28 years old. She is a very attractive girl with fair complexion. She is the only daughter of her parents. She has a very cheerful disposition and keeps the moods alive in any gathering with her quick wit. She is also physically strong. Her parents arranged her marriage. But her husband's income of Rs.2,000 is less than her earnings. The income of her husband was low and inadequate to manage the family. The marital life was also dull without any excitement. A year after her marriage she gave birth to a son. She had to depend on her brother to buy clothes. She knows that her parents will not take care of her anymore. She took a decision to join work after her neighbor friend advised about this job. And she joined this job after the paper notification. She lives in a kaccha rented house near the Zone. Including her, there are three members in the family. Her husband has also permitted her to join this job. Then she took up the job in 1998. Originally the family is from Eluru in West Godavari District. She received training from the company for six months. She earns Rs.5,500 as salary per month. The status of her economic condition is very low before she took up this job. After completing the household chores in the morning, Chaitanya goes to duty with her husband. The income from their jobs has brought about a vast change in the lifestyle of the couple. She feels proud to say that her husband has brought a bike for Rs.2,500. They buy house appliances with their own money. Moreover both have the habit of watching movies. They plan to buy a black and white television set next year, if they manage to save enough money. The couple spends their leisure time with their son. She also conducts tuitions for intermediate students in the holidays. The reason behind entering this job was her financial condition. Now she overcomes economic problems and is independent earner. Currently her husband is very proud of his wife.

Because of the work, she suffers from burning sensation in the eyes and headache. She suggests that company must improve working environment of women workers. Medical aid, medical check-ups, prevention methods, must be improved by the company to increase their job satisfaction and working capacity. This is a case study of a young married couple that works together in their own jobs, manages the family and saves money that can be used for some luxuries.

SECTION -III

5.4 Levels of Living

It may be pertinent to enquire as to what would be the levels of living of the women workers in the VSEZ units. The income of the respondents is added to the income of the head of the household to assess the level of living.

TABLE-5.5

Average Family Income of Women Workers in the VSEZ.

Category of Workers	Respondent's Income	Income of other than the Respondents	Total family Income
WWD	381400 (51.09)	365100 (48.91)	746500 (100.00)
MKW	126700 (45.61)	151100 (54.39)	277800 (100.00)
BSW	147300 (48.25)	158000 (51.75)	305300 (100.00)
LID	248800 (44.68)	308000 (55.32)	556800 (100.00)
Total	904200 (47.93)	982200 (52.07)	1886400 (100.00)

Table 5.5 shows the average income of the family. It could be observed from the Table that the contribution of women in family's income for the total sample is 48 per cent. Across the sub units the share of women earner in the monthly family income is the highest in case of the WWD unit (51 per cent) and the lowest in case of the LID unit (45 per cent). The share in case of the MKW unit (46 per cent) and the BSW unit (48 per cent) also low. It could be said that the total monthly family

income as shown in the Table should give them a level of living above the poverty line.

However, it needs to be examined whether they are really above poverty line in terms of the family expenditure. It could further be observed from Table 5.6.

TABLE-5.6

Average Income and Expenditure at the Household level.

Category of Workers	Total family Income	Total Expenditure	(Col.3) as % of (Col.2)
WWD	746500	550100	73.69
MKW	277800	221400	79.70
BSW	305300	235600	77.17
LID	556800	423100	75.99
Total	1886400	1430200	75.82

The above Table 5.6 observed that 75.81 per cent of the income is spent in the case of total women workers. In the case of the WWD workers it was 73.69 per cent, the MKW workers spent 79.69 per cent, the LID workers spent 77.17 per cent and the BSW workers spent 75.98 per cent of their income and the remaining percentage of income goes to savings. The savings are mostly used to meet social functions and other obligations. The investment of savings in assets is mostly in the form of gold, postal savings and shares.

5.5 Conclusion

It could be summarised that the women workers in the SEZ units in Visakhapatnam city are supporting their families bringing in almost half the family income. With the help of multiple regressions, the determinants of income of the women workers were analysed. Education, age, marital status and experience could be considered as significant variables explaining income variations. The determinants of income may not be same across the four units of women workers in the present study. The regression results relating to WWD unit indicate that the coefficient of R^2 is consistently positive in all the equations.

Is could thus be concluded that habits of the head of the household, absence of male head in families and social obligations seem to be obstructing the people in the VSEZ units to live above the poverty line, although they have 'entitlement' in terms of income.

References:

[1] Mincer, J. (1974): *Schooling, Experience and earning*, NBER, New York.

[2] Mohan, R. (1981): "The Determinants and Labour Earnings in Developing Metropolies--- Estimates from Bagota", Kali Colombia, *World Bank Staff Working Paper*, No.498, Washington D.C.

[3] Mazumdar, T. (1979): "Paradigms in the study of urban Markets in LDC's – A measurement in the light of an empirical survey in Bambay city", *World Bank Staff Working Paper*, No.366, Washington D.C.

[4] Mazumdar, D. and Ahmad, M. (1978): "Labour Market segmentation and determination of earnings", *World Bank Staff Working Paper*, No. 278, Washington.

[5] Murthy, K.S. (1986): "Urbain Labour Informal Sector-A Case Study of Visakhapatnam City", B.R.P.C., Delhi, p.98.

[6] Carbo, V. and Steloner (1983): "Earnings Determination and Labour Market", *Journal of Development Economics*, Vol, 12, p. 266.

CHAPTER - VI

CHAPTER - VI

MIGRATION OF WOMEN WORKERS IN THE VSEZ

6.1 Introduction:

The determinants of income of women workers in the VSEZ are analysed in the previous Chapter. In this Chapter an attempt is made to examine socio-economic conditions of the migrants among women workers in the VSEZ. This Chapter is divided into two Sections. Section -- I deals with the meaning, concept, types and causes of migration. Section – II presents socio-economic conditions of migrants in the EPZs.

SECTION - I

An attempt is made in this Section to give the meaning of the concept, types and causes of migration.

6.2 Meaning:

In physiological terms migration primarily means movement of people from one place or location to another, which is not of a casual nature, as a visit or a tour. Migration is necessarily a pre-emptive move; it is the survival instinct that drives humans to seek better prospects. It is generally believed that the process of globalisation all over the world has accelerated the migration trend, particularly of women in search of survival, fulfillment and a better life for themselves and their families. Recent studies in India have reported an increasing number of young women joining the migrant flow to cities, many of them going on their own to find work in service industry, manufacturing and informal sectors. Many scholars have analysed the phenomenon of migration, but it is only since the 1970s that scholars have made attempts to understand migration from a gender perspective on account of the realisation that there are gender related variations in the causes, consequences and patterns of migration[1].

Phizlackea (1996) points to three contemporary economic sectors, which indicate a peculiar model of current female migratory processes: the sex and marriage industries, the maid industry and the home working of migrant and ethnic minority women. The Italian example fits this model, as a large proportion of migrant women are employed as domestic workers. Female migrant labour offers specific advantages to employers they can be employed in certain low wage sectors of the economy.

Black women's migration to Italy as primary migrants provides new evidence of a shift in women's migratory patterns, i.e., feminisation of migration[2]. Women make up nearly half of the international migrant population. In all countries more men than women appear to be migrating, although the women migrating in India outnumber males. In India, men dominate migration streams to large cities, but women dominate in short distance moves within the rural areas. The latter trend reflects mainly marriage migration, where the Indian custom requires that the bride move to the husband's village. More than 75 per cent of all migrants in India are women[3]

Migration, a complex multivariate phenomenon, is both cause and consequence of various social, cultural and economic constraints as experienced by the people in the society. It has varying degrees of impact both at the origin and destination points[4]. Migration in India is a caste / class neutral process; it takes place in rich as well as poor classes. Rural elites migrate to the city for advanced education and subsequently take up urban jobs, adding to the family's wealth. They provide the capitalist base for agriculture to the parent family[5]. On the other hand, poor peasants and tenants, landless labourers, marginal groups and poor artisans migrate to the big villages, towns and cities in order to avoid unemployment. Development planning and the processes of modernisation and urbanisation have affected the life and the work of the people significantly, particularly in the rural areas. Some recent studies have disclosed that a significant proportion of female migration in India takes place for economic reasons and therefore, there is a closer analysis of the pattern of employment of the migrant women in the changed circumstances. While economic factors are obviously basic to migration decisions, socio-cultural factors shape the migration stream in the Indian setting. The act of migration is viewed as a collective strategy adjusting the household unit to external changes in the productive system[6].

The Committee on the Status of Women has raised many questions relating to migrant women and a need for detailed investigation of the impact of broken marriages, widowhood, desertion and abandonment of women on migration. Such women may be migrating in order to earn their livelihood[7]. Similarly, social and cultural factors related to caste and religions have important implications for decisions to migrate or not to migrate and for the consequences of migration for women, especially in terms of their pattern of workforce participation in the city[8].

6.2.1 The Concept of Migration:

Migration means a change in, or shift, other than casual, of residence from one location or settlement to another involving movement across an administrative border. The administrative border may be that of a village, district or state or nation. In fact, there is no universally applicable definition for migration[9]. The term "migration" has been defined as "the act or an instance of moving from one country, region or place to settle in another in search of work"[10]. Peterson views migration as movement motivated by the individual willingness to risk the unknown of a new home and breaking from a familiar social universe for the sake of adventure, achievement of ideals or to escape a social system from which he has become alienated[11]. According to Keneth Kamneyer, "migration is a relatively permanent moving away of collectively called migrants from one geographical location to another, preceded by decision making on the part of the migrants on the basis of hierarchically ordered set of values or value ends and resulting in changes in the international system of the migration[12]. According to United Nations "migration is a form of geographical mobility or spatial mobility, between one geographical unit and another, generally involving a change in residence from the place of origin or place of departure to the place of destination or place of arrival".

Theadore Caplow states that "Migration is strictly speaking a change of residence and need not necessarily involve only change of occupational shifts of one kind or another"[13]. He further states that "certain constants may be observed at once wherever migration tends to flow from areas of high fertility to areas of low fertility, and in the direction of economic opportunity"[14].

Thus migration is viewed as a shift from one place to another to avoid the social and demographic problems and seek better economic opportunities, ultimately leading to social change.

6.2.2 Types of Migration:

Three types of migration are normally considered:

1. Permanent,
2. Seasonal and
3. Half seasonal.

Migration between one geographical unit and another, generally involving a change in residence from the place of origin or place of departure to the place of destination or place of arrival irrespective of the distance involved is called permanent migration.

In the case of seasonal migration the migrants like agricultural labour and marginal farmers go to nearby towns for work during off season and return to village in peak agricultural season. In this case village is their permanent residence[15].

Half-seasonal migration represents migration of rural poor (landless agricultural workers, marginal farmers and others) at the time of flood, drought and other natural calamities to safer places. They return to their native places after the natural calamity is over[16].

6.2.3 Causes for Migration:

Economic and non-economic factors are identified as causes of migration.

6.2.3.1 Economic Factors:

Agriculture happens to be a backward sector in most of the developing countries. Insufficiency of cultivable land, lack of irrigation facilities and low rate of investment in agriculture has contributed to lower stagnant growth of income. Fragmentation and subdivision of land ownership due to increasing pressure of population resulting in high indebtedness, inequality in the distribution of land and other productive assets further worsened the levels of living in the rural sector. These causes constitute the push factors[17].

Industrialisation and thereby creation of better employment opportunities, comforts available in urban life, lack of jobs in rural areas to commensurate with educational qualifications act as urban pull factors.

6.2.3.2 Non-Economic Factors:

Family disputes, attractiveness of city life, commercial fairs, wars and famines, family size and its structure, social factors outside their village such as educational prospects for children, entertainment opportunities strongly contribute to migration. Presence of friends and relatives in towns help in getting jobs and political factors may hasten migration.

Thus migration implies that generally able-bodied people in the working age group in search of higher income opportunities migrate. Such migration is usually from rural to urban areas as industrialisation with its higher income earning opportunities is concentrated in the urban areas. Further, migration may or may not change occupational structure of the migrants. Income may increase after migration but it is difficult to conclude that the general level of living of migrants gets enhanced which depends not only on income but on the availability of basic amenities[18].

SECTION –II

In this Section socio-economic conditions of the migrants in EPZs are observed in brief.

6.3 Women Migration in the EPZs

In the late 1950's and 1960's the preponderance of women migrating to urban areas indicated the essential economic motive for migration probably for temporary duration. The gradual increase in women migrants reflected an acknowledgment of the need or desire of an extended stay due to economic pressure.

Migration of poor families from countryside to urban cities in search of livelihood and employment is a regular phenomenon in the economic life of India. The backwardness in the agriculture, lack of irrigation facilities and famines have made hazardous effect on the income and lives of poor peasants and landless agricultural labourers and the result is unending migration to the towns in search of better life.

Women are also part of those poor families who experienced the sorts of hardships along with men and in few cases women exclusively are found migrating to other areas leaving their parents, husbands and children at native village.

There has been significant empirical evidence on women's work and their migration. In the traditional rural sector, women significantly work as 'free wage labourers' or permanently bandaged labour and the income derived thereby are insignificant. Further seasonal fluctuations in employment are high for women. Various socio-economic, cultural and psychological factors hinder the development of women. In such a situation women migrate in search of better income earning opportunities and thereby better level of living.

Poverty stricken unemployed, in the absence of no other means of survival, is forced to move to place where there is 'availability of jobs' based on casual information and speculation on wage and work situations. Migrant women are preferred in almost all the fish processing industry in India[19]. It is because migrant women are powerless and atomised, often working through contractors, unaware of legal rights, deprived of even basic recognition from society or trade unions as workers entitled to minimum wages and inferior working conditions[20].

Predominance of migrant women is the unique feature of the Visakhapatnam Special Economic Zone (VSEZ). Data relating to the migrants and non-migrants of women workers are presented in Table 6.1.

TABLE - 6.1

Migrants and Non-Migrants of Women Workers in the VSEZ Units

S. No	Category of Workers	VSEZ Units					Per cent
		WWD	MKW	BSW	LID	Total	
1	Migrants	93 (43.06)	39 (18.06)	34 (15.74)	50 (23.15)	216	69.45
2	Non-Migrants	10 (10.53)	13 (13.68)	19 (20.00)	53 (55.79)	95	30.55
	Total	103	52	53	103	311	
	Per cent	33.12	16.72	17.04	33.12		100.00

Source: Data collected from the Office of the VSEZ, Visakhapatnam.

As shown Ante Italics.

Note: Figures in the parenthesis indicate percentages

Migrants and Non-Migrants of Women workers in the VSEZ units are presented in Table 6.1. It shows that 69 per cent of the respondents are migrants; highest percent of migrant respondents are working in the WWD followed by the LID, the MKW and the BSW. Alternatively the percent of non-migrants is highest in the LID, followed by the BSW, the MKW and the WWD.

TABLE - 6.2

Distance of Migration among Women Workers in the VSEZ Units

S. No	Place	VSEZ Units					Per cent
		WWD	MKW	BSW	LID	Total	
1	Within Mandal	35 (42.17)	10 (12.05)	15 (18.07)	23 (27.71)	83	38.43
2	Within District	37 (47.05)	19 (22.62)	12 (14.29)	16 (19.05)	84	38.89
3	Within the State	19 (40.43)	10 (21.28)	07 (14.89)	11 (23.40)	47	21.76
4	Neighboring State	01 (100.00)	0	0	0	01	0.46
5	Faraway Place	01 (100.00)	0	0	0	01	0.46
	Total	93	39	34	50	216	
	Per cent	43.06	18.06	15.74	23.14		100.0

Note: Figures in the parenthesis indicate percentages

Table-6.2 presents Distance of Migration among Women Workers in the VSEZ units. It shows the origin of migrants from which they migrated. It is observed from the Table that among the respondents 38 per cent of migrants are from the same Mandal. Another 38.89 per cent are from the same district; nearly 22 per cent of the migrants are from the same State. One or two migrants are from neighboring States or from far away places. In the case of the WWD unit migrant workers are very high when compared to other units.

TABLE - 6.3

Migrants by Family Occupation at the Origin

Sl. No	Type of Occupation	VSEZ Units					Per Cent
		WWD	MKW	BSW	LID	Total	
1	Wage Labour	30	25	20	48	123	39.55
		(29.13)	(48.08)	(37.74)	(46.60)		
2	Agricultural Labour	26	13	18	22	79	25.40
		(25.24)	(25.00)	(33.96)	(21.36)		
3	Business	22	06	09	17	54	17.36
		(21.36)	(11.54)	(16.98)	(16.50)		
4	Tailoring	17	05	04	11	37	11.90
		(16.50)	(9.62)	(7.55)	(10.68)		
5	No Work	08	03	02	05	18	5.79
		(7.77)	(5.77)	(3.77)	(4.85)		
	Total	103	52	53	103	311	-
	Percentage	100.00	100.00	100.00	100.00	-	100.0

Note: Figures in the parenthesis indicate percentages

Table 6.3 presents the Migrants by family occupation at the origin. It can be observed from the Table that the significant proportion (39.55 per cent) of the workers were wage labourers before migration. Another 25 per cent of the workers were agricultural labourers, followed by business and tailoring with 17.36 and 11.90 respectively. Nearly six per cent of the workers were unemployed before migration. Migrants of family occupation among four units of the VSEZ show the similar trend as in the total migrants of all units. The proportion of the migrants is significant from wage labourers followed by agricultural labourers, business and tailoring.

TABLE - 6.4

Reasons for Migration among Women Workers in the VSEZ Units

S. No	Reasons for Migration	VSEZ Units					Per cent
		WWD	MKW	BSW	LID	Total	
1	Father / Mother	36 (38.71)	15 (38.46)	18 (52.94)	30 (60.0)	99	45.83
2	Husband	37 (39.78)	15 (38.46)	11 (32.35)	13 (26.0)	76	35.19
3	Brother (s)	5 (5.38)	0	1 (2.94)	5 (10.0)	11	5.09
4	Sister (s)	6 (6.45)	3 (7.69)	2 (5.88)	0	11	5.09
5	Friends	4 (4.30)	1 (2.56)	0	0	5	2.31
6	Relatives	1 (1.08)	4 (10.26)	2 (5.88)	2 (4.0)	9	4.18
7	Others	4 (4.30)	1 (2.56)	0	0	5	2.31
	Total	93	39	34	50	216	
	Per cent	100	100	100	100		100

Note: Figures in the parenthesis indicate percentages

Table 6.4 shows reasons for migration of migrants. It observed from the Table that the proportion of the migrant respondents migrated along with their father or mother who migrated in search of work is 45.83 per cent. The proportion of the migrants who migrated along with their husbands account for 35.19. The proportions of the other reasons for migration are brother, sister, friends, relatives etc., are insignificant.

TABLE - 6.5

Duration of Immigration of Women Workers in the VSEZ Units

S. No	Duration (in Years)	VSEZ Units					Per cent
		WWD	MKW	BSW	LID	Total	
1	< 5	45 (48.39)	27 (69.23)	20 (58.82)	37 (74.00)	129	59.72
2	6 – 10	35 (37.63)	7 (17.95)	9 (26.47)	6 (12.00)	57	26.39
3	11 – 15	8 (8.60)	5 (12.82)	5 (14.71)	3 (6.00)	21	9.72
4	16 – 20	5 (5.38)	0	0	2 (4.00)	7	3.24
5	> 21	0	0	0	2 (4.00)	2	0.93
	Total	93	39	34	50	216	
	Per cent	100.00	100.00	100.00	100.00		100

Note: Figures in the parenthesis indicate percentages

Table 6.5 represents the data on the duration of residence of immigrants of the VSEZ units. Among the total respondents the proportion of the workers has been in the city for less than five years account for nearly 60 per cent and 26.39 per cent of workers have been in the city between 6-10 years. All together 86 per cent of migrants have been residing on the city for less than 10 years. Only around 14 per cent of the migrants are residing in the city for more than 10 years.

TABLE - 6.6

Type of Living Conditions (residence) of Women Workers in the VSEZ Units.

S. No	Type of House	VSEZ Units WWD	MKW	BSW	LID	Total	Per cent
1	Concrete	30 (29.13)	11 (21.15)	10 (18.87)	20 (19.42)	71	22.83
2	Thatched	41 (39.81)	27 (51.92)	23 (43.40)	45 (43.69)	136	43.73
3	Hut	32 (31.07)	14 (26.92)	20 (37.74)	38 (36.89)	104	33.44
	Total	103	52	53	103	311	
	Per cent	100.00	100.00	100.00	100.00		100

Note: Figures in the parenthesis indicate percentages

Table 6.6 shows the type of living conditions (residence) of the respondents. The Table reveals that majority of the respondents' families are living in thatched houses (43.73 per cent), followed by huts (33.44 per cent), only 22.83 per cent of the total respondents are living in concrete houses. It infers that there is need for the construction of concrete houses for workers by the management of the VSEZ to improve the living conditions of the workers. Otherwise it is suggested to provide HRA (House Rent Allowance) as an incentive to the workers.

TABLE - 6.7

House Ownership Status of Women Workers in the VSEZ Units

S. No	Type of Status	VSEZ Units					Per cent
		WWD	MKW	BSW	LID	Total	
1	Own	32 (31.07)	24 (46.15)	20 (37.74)	45 (43.69)	121	38.9
2	Rented	44 (42.72)	25 (48.08)	28 (52.83)	50 (48.54)	147	47.27
3	Others	27 (26.21)	3 (5.77)	5 (9.43)	8 (7.77)	43	13.83
	Total	103	52	53	103	311	
	Per cent	100.00	100.00	100.00	100.00		100

Note: Figures in the parenthesis indicate percentages

Table 6.7 shows the house ownership status of women workers in the VSEZ units. Regarding the house ownership status 38.9 per cent of the total respondents are having own houses and 47.27 per cent of the respondents residing in rented houses. Some of the total respondents 13.83 per cent are residing in hostels, friends' houses or with relatives.

TABLE - 6.8

Income (per month) of Women Workers in the VSEZ Units

S. No	Income (in Rupees p.m)	VSEZ Units					Per cent
		WWD	MKW	BSW	LID	Total	
1	< 2000	10 (9.71)	22 (42.31)	18 (33.96)	51 (49.51)	101	32.48
2	2001 - 3000	24 (23.30)	19 (36.54)	16 (30.19)	30 (29.13)	89	28.62
3	3001 - 4000	31 (30.10)	8 (15.38)	13 (24.53)	16 (15.53)	68	21.86
4	4001 - 5000	29 (28.16)	3 (5.77)	4 (7.55)	4 (3.88)	40	12.86
5	> 5001	9 (8.74)	0	2 (3.77)	2 (1.94)	13	4.18
	Total	103	52	53	103	311	
	Per cent	100.00	100.00	100.00	100.00		100

Figures in the parenthesis indicate percentages

The data relating to earnings of selected women workers in the sampled units of the VSEZ is grouped into five categories and these respective data are presented in Table 6.8. It is observed from the Table that 32.48 per cent of women workers fall in the category of income less than Rs.2000/- per month followed by income between rupees Rs.2001-3000 per month (28.62 per cent), income between Rs.3001-4000 per month (21.86 per cent) and income between Rs.4001-5000 per month (12.86 per cent). Only 4.18 per cent of women workers are drawing more than Rs.5, 000/- per month. It is further observed from the Table that on the whole more than 60 per cent of the women workers are drawing the salary / wage less than Rs.3000/-.

6.4 Summary:

Skeldon argues that the movement of population can be a significant factor for the alleviation of poverty (2002:75). This may partly hold well in case of international migration, but in the Indian context this cannot be an appropriate solution. Secondly it depends on how one perceives poverty. If it is defined in a narrow economic sense of low levels of income then migration may help in poverty eradication. In a broader perspective of human development, which embraces better quality of life with access to basic necessities, migration cannot be considered as promoting human development. Migration is perceived by governments, policy-makers and urban planners in India as undesirable. In cities, the population living in squatter and in slum settlement is showing an upward trend and the mushrooming growth of slum population exerts increased pressure on provision of minimum basic services such as housing, water supply, health, education and other basic infrastructure including sanitation. Supply of these services is one of the biggest challenges to all urban planners and policymakers[21].

Some results were observed in this Study, besides above problems in the VSEZ units 69.45 per cent are migrant women and a majority of them belong to within the district (38.89 per cent). The proportion of migrants is significant from wage labourers followed by agricultural labourers, business and tailoring. The proportion of the migrants respondents migrated with their father/mother is highest to the per cent of 45.83. All together 86 per cent of migrants have been residing in the city for less than 10 years. On an average migrant workers are having more family income. The housing details show that majority is living in thatched houses (43.73 per cent), with regard to house ownership status; migrant workers have no better status. Altogether, it appears that these women workers belong to lower middle-income group and there are no significant differences between local and migrant women workers with respect to socio-economic characteristics. It was found that the migrant women worked in the VSEZ units with out any legal protection or job security, with long hours, low wages and no facilities at all. The migrant women are working under bad sanitary and unsafe conditions.

The Study suggests that there is need for construction of concrete houses by the management to improve the living conditions of the workers in the VSEZ, otherwise, to provide house rent allowance as an incentive to the workers.

CHART-6.1 UNIT-WISE DISTRIBUTION OF SAMPLE RESPONDENTS BY THIER NATIVITY

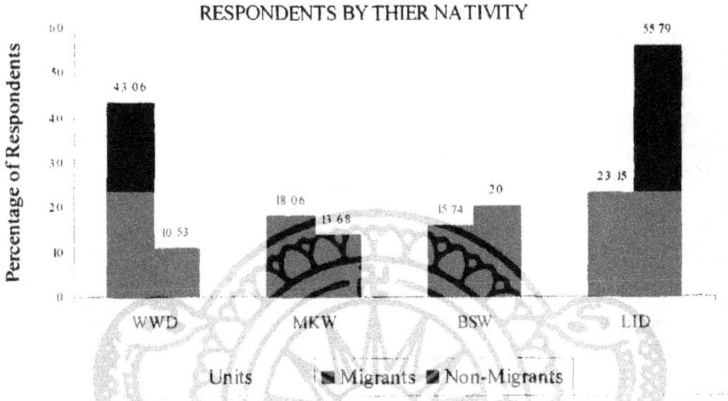

CHART-6.2 UNIT-WISE DISTRIBUTION OF SAMPLE RESPONDENTS BY THIER PLACE OF MIGRATION

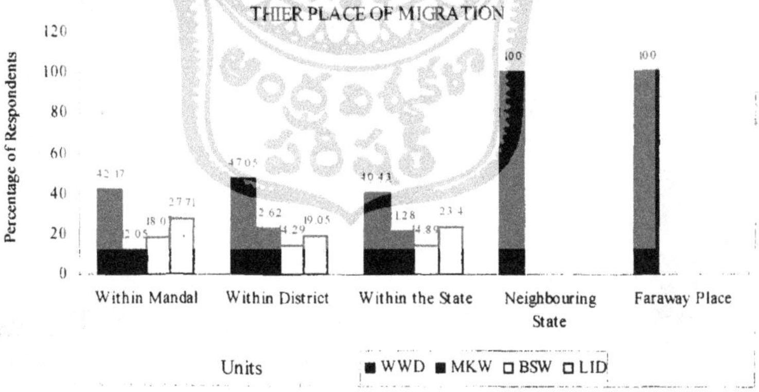

CHART-6.3 DISTRIBUTION OF MIGRANT WOMEN WORKERS BY THIER OCCUPATION

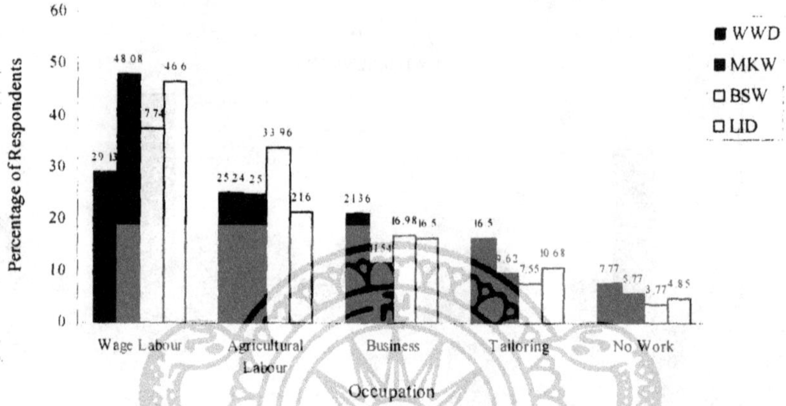

CHART-6.4 DISTRIBUTION OF WOMEN WORKERS BY REASONS FOR MIGRATION

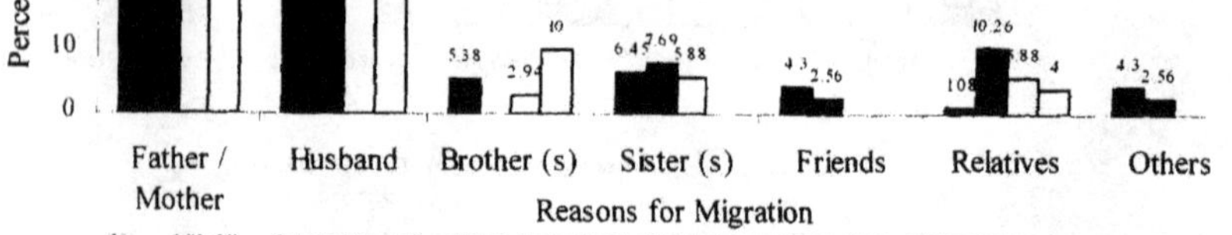

CHART-6.5 DISTRIBUTION OF WOMEN WORKERS BY DURATION OF MIGRATION

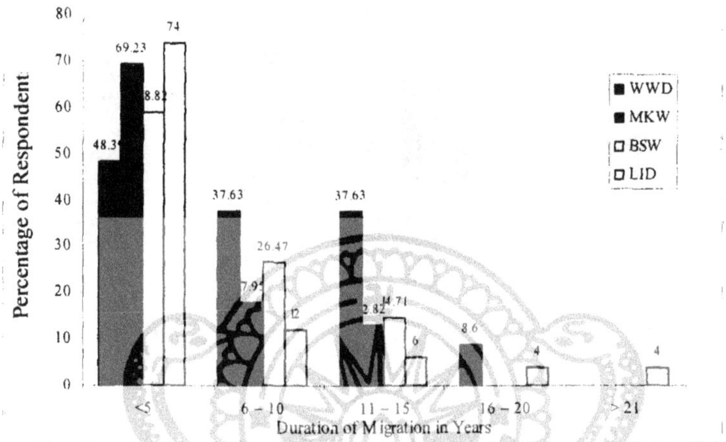

CHART-6.6 DISTRIBUTION OF WOMEN WORKERS BY TYPE OF HOUSE

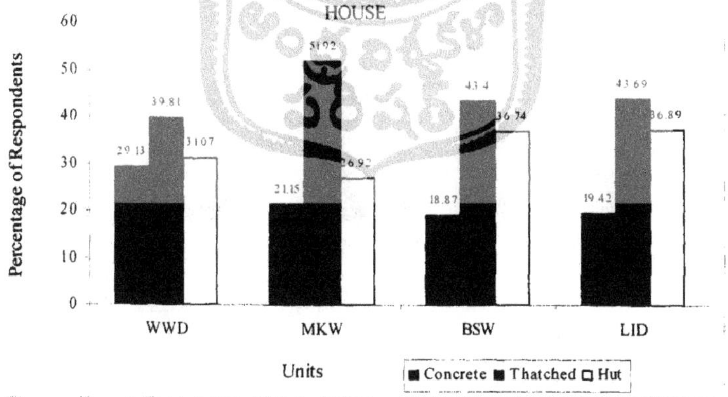

CHART-6.7 DISTRIBUTION OFWOMEN WORKERS BY TUPE OF STATUS

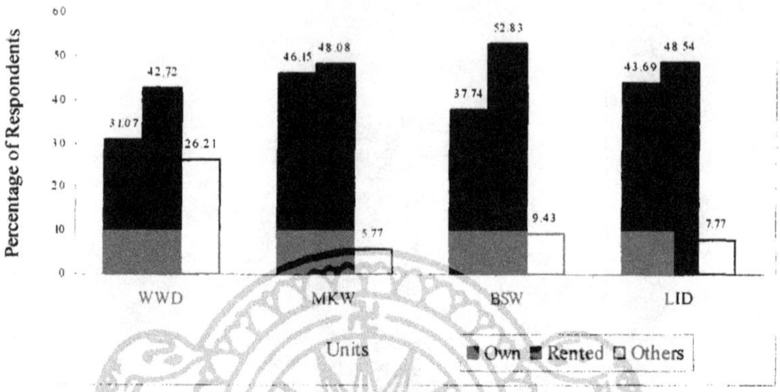

CHART-6.8 DISTRIBUTION OF WOMEN WORKERS BY THIER INCOME

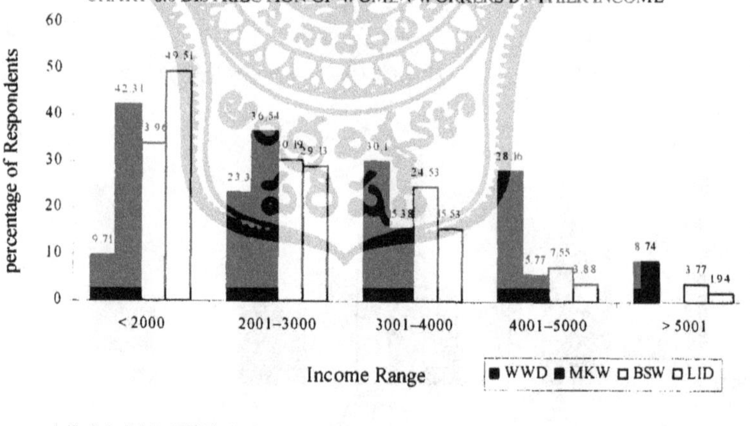

References:

[1] S.Sundari (2005): "Migration as a Livelihood Strategy A Gender Perspective" *Economic and Political Weekly,* May 28, Vol.XL, No.23 & 24, June 4, p. 2295.

[2] Andall and Jacqueline (2000): *Gender, Migration and Domestic Service,* Ashgate, US.

[3] Government of India (2000): *National Sample Survey Consumption Expenditure Data (55th Round, 1999-2000),* Planning Commission, New Delhi.

[4] Divya and Pandey (1993): *Migrant Labour and Gender Dimension-Micro Analysis of Gender Differentials in Migrant Workers,* Research Centre for Women's Studies, S.N.D.T. Women' University, Mumbai.

[5] Rao, D.V. (1992): *Status of Women and Children in Slums: A study of Hyderabad City,* Navrang, New Delhi.

[6] Wood, C. (1981): Structural Change and Household Strategies: A Conceptual Framework for the Study of Rural Migration, *Human Organisation,* 40 (4), pp.338-344.

[7] Government of India (1974): *Towards Equality: Report of the Committee on the Status of women in India,* New Delhi, Department of Social Welfare.

[8] Singh, A.M. (1978): "Rural Urban Migration of Women among the Urban Poor in India: Causes and Consequences, *Social Action,* 28 (4), pp.326-236.

[9] Thomas, D.S. (1993): "Research Memorandum on Migration Differentials", *Social Science Research Council Bulletin,* 43, New York, p.4.

[10] Webster: *Third New International Dictionary,* Marsealers g. 8c Marisions Co., Vol.III, P.1432.

[11] Peterson and William (1958): "A General Typology of Migration", *American Studies Review*, Vol.23, June, p.256.

[12] Kenneth Kamneyer (1975): *Population Studies Selected Essays and Research*. Chicago, p.175.

[13] Theador Caplow (1954): *The sociology of work*, the University of Minnesota Press, Minneopolis, p. 60.

[14] Ibid. p.88.

[15] Everetts Lee (1975): *Theory of Migration*, Kenneth, U.K. Kamneyer (ed.,), p.191.

[16] Ibid.

[17] The following studies may be as important in this regard.

a) Morali Monohar, K. (1983): *Social Economic States of Indian Women*, p.10.

b) Aziz Abdul (1983): *Urban Poor and Urban Informal Sector*, p.22.

c) Mazumdar, D.N. (1960): *Social Contours of an Industrial City*, Asia Publishing House, Bombay, p.73.

d) Mishra and Sridar (1952): "Urban Employment and Migration of Agriculture Labour in U.P." *Rural India*, 15 (3), March.

e) Standing,G.and Skedeo, F : "Labour Migration and Development in Gayana" in *International Labour Review*, Nov.- Dec., Vol. 116, No. 3, pp.303-313.

f) Griffen, K (1974): *Land Concentration and Rural Poverty*, London, McMillan.

g) Kingsley Danis (1950): *The Population of India and Pakisthan*, p.108.

[18] The importance studies are:

a) Kingsley Danis (1950): *The Population of India and Pakistan*, Princeton, New Jersey.

b) Gupta,O.P (1972): "Volume, Factors and Characteristics of Migration to Urban Delhi", *Indian Census Centenary Seminar*, Vol.1, Office of the Registrar-General of India. Ministry of Home Affairs, New Delhi, p. 69.

c) Ganguli, B.N (1973): *Population and Development*, S. Chand & Co. Pvt. Ltd., New Delhi, p.54.

d) John Connel and Biplab Das Gupta (1976): *Migration from Rural Areas*, Oxford University Press, Delhi, pp.38-53.

[19] Patel G.Harbhai (1987): "Kerala Migrant Female Labour in Fishing units of Viraval City of Western India" in Vidyut Joshi (Ed) *Migrant Labour abd Related Issues*, Oxford & IBH Publishing Co. Pvt. Ltd., Gandhi Labour Institute, Ahmadabad.

[20] Surinder Jetley (1990): "Women in the food Processing Industry" in Divya Pandey & Mira Savara (ed.), *Between the Farm and Thali – Women in Food Processing*, Research Centre for Women Studies, S.N.D.T. Women's University, Mumbai, p.91.

[21] Skeldon and Ronald (1997): "Rural-urban Migration and Its Implications for Poverty Alleviation", *Asia-Pacific Population Journal*, 12 (1).

CHAPTER - VIII

CHAPTER-VII
SUMMARY AND CONCLUSION

This Chapter presents the results of the Study along with their policy implications for further research. The Study throws new light for an objective understanding of social reality in the problem area.

7.1 Objective of the Study:

… socio-economi… …sing the employ… …esides a Study … …ers and thereaft… …lift the standar… …ofile of the wo… …ers, the Study n… …terns of both th… …working conditi…

T… against the backdrop of the history of SEZs, the role and significance of Indian SEZs and contain the objectives of the Study, data base, methodology and methodological problems. The second Chapter presents a review of the literature and the third Chapter is devoted to the socio-economic profile of the women workers in VSEZ. The fourth Chapter deals with the employment, health and working environment of women workers in VSEZ units. The fifth Chapter contains determinants of income of women workers in units and the sixth Chapter analyses the migration of women workers. This chapter presents the summary and policy implications of the Study.

7.2 Major Findings:

Though a major proportion of workforce in EPZs is women, unfortunately their economic importance is not recognised and the jobs they do are always unskilled or low skilled. It may be noted that many of the employers are reluctant to invest in developing the skills of women as they feel it as a waste of investment but still they have a strong preference for women workers because of their dexterity, patience and other specific attributes which make them more suitable than men for carrying out tasks that demand painstaking attention to detail and are repetitive. Regardless of their level of education, women constitute the bulk of unskilled and semi-skilled workforce especially in textiles, clothing, leather, electronics and diamond industries. Throughout the country, EPZs have revealed a strong preference for the female workers just like in other countries. The exploitation of women in these zones is very apparent when one considers the work culture, stubborn employee relations of the management in terms of leave and rigid shift policies and lack of other basic facilities. Most of the women, about 70 per cent, are young and unmarried and are from rural areas with poor economic background. But surprisingly, the educational background of the women had not affected the income-earning capacity of the workers or the productivity. The turnover of this labour force is continuous to EPZs. Employers look to extract long hours of uninterrupted work and prefer young and unmarried women who have least family responsibilities. In some units, women are not allowed to use the toilet while work is pending and many units do not pay full salary for maternity leave. Sexual harassment and lack of transport facilities, especially for women working in the night shifts are the other problems faced by the women employees of these units. Long hours of work in a standing posture and dust pollution are the other areas which cause concern regarding the health of the women workers.

Since the workers are drawn mainly from the rural unskilled female category, they learn the skills through work under a supervisor for a period of time and specific training programmes are also conducted by the managements. While some units have one-year training, others have only for six months. Employees, who undergo training, in turn impart the skills to less experienced co-workers. In case of under performance a second term of training is provided to help them graduate to the permanent category. Skill development through "learning by doing" continues at other stages of operation as well.

EPZs have achieved their objective of promoting exports but they failed to meet the objectives of improving the welfare and working environment of women workers. Hence, policy intervention through guidelines and support structures are necessary to improve the employment conditions of women workers which can stop or reduce the exploitation in these units.

The wage structure has to be revised and payments for over-time should be enhanced. Night-shift allowance and provision for basic facilities would go a long way in improving the lot of the women workers.

India is one of the pioneers in the world in making a policy decision regarding Free Trade Zones way back in early sixties and the country is the first in Asia to start a zone which came up in Kandla in 1965. The Visakhapatnam Export Processing Zone (VEPZ), which later became VSEZ, is one of the governmental organizations established in the year 1989 in an area of 366 acres with an aim of promoting export oriented goods and services. It became operational in mid nineties and presently has 20 units which provide employment to 2692, of which 1090 are women making up 40.49 per cent of the workforce. The high percentage of the presence of women workers indicates a strong preference for women workers by the employers. Most of the women are found in textile, clothing, leather, electronics and diamond establishments.

Due to modern technology, non-militant nature, steady and sincere workforce and low wages for female labour, the preference for female workforce has gone up. The introduction of female labour started in early 1980s because of these factors and employment opportunities for women increased in these units by 20 per cent within a span of 50 years. Though there is no strict division of labour on the basis of gender, women are mostly employed in the EPZs particularly in select industries mentioned earlier due to their trustworthiness, sincerity and steadiness. The other reasons like increase in import and export activities have also contributed to the steady increase of women workforce.

Today, because of the national need, the changing pattern of society and the desire to contribute towards the general good, and their own satisfaction and economic relief, women are emerging in various fields of services. Because of their increasing numbers as workers outside the home, world organisations, such as the International Labour Organisation, National Government and competent authorities are concentrating themselves more and more on the special problems, which married women with family responsibilities face and in giving them equal opportunities. The consensus of opinion now is that it is almost inevitable that women will work, no matter what the motivation is, and they should be helped by the society as a whole so that the hitherto dormant women power can be harnessed to make women an integrated part of a stable working force.

The changing world has brought many new interests into women's orbit and altered the pattern of domestic life. India is a developing country and as such its women do not take enough active part in the economic reconstruction of their motherland.

However, community policies and public opinion has to be created to help women to meet their multiple duties. Regarding re-entry into employment after childbirth, the employment policy convention 1964 and ILO advocate that women be a part of the integrated labour force on equal footing with men. In 1951 a convention concerning equal remuneration for men and women workers of equal value was adopted by the ILO and was ratified by India. The Planning Commission for the third plan period stated that "there will be need for a large number of women workers in various spheres of activity".

However, though opportunities for female labour force increased steadily, it led to their exploitation too. The women employers in EPZs, particularly in diamond and knitwear industries, suffer from problems ranging from insecurity of employment, lack of standard minimum wages, excessive hours of work and absence of welfare amenities.

Though there are laws to enforce regular payment and prevention of unfair deduction of wages, provision of regular working hours, laws and holidays, proper environment, supply of drinking water and social security against old age, sickness in human working conditions, low trade unions etc. there is no effective government machinery to monitor the implementation of these laws in the interest of workers in general and women in particular in these units in the VSEZ. A particular study has shown 100 types of harassments in VSEZ. The Study has identified, among others, that there are no festival holidays, no over-time wages, and no maternity leave. An incident of a Christian worker being suspended for availing leave on a Christmas day and the suspension of two workers who took the 'Ayyappa Deeksha' were examples of the treatment meted out to women workers. In another case, a woman was terminated immediately after her pregnancy was known. Illegal deduction from salary, for petty reasons like being active in union, for not drinking tea, for moving the stool, for casting vote in local body elections, show the mean mentality of the management and the severe nature of exploitation as the workforce has no voice.

It would not be out of place here to briefly look into what Smt. T K Rajalakshmi wrote. She was awarded the Panos Reproductive Health Media Fellowship in 1998 and in an article she gave a graphic account of life at an export processing zone near Delhi where workers pay a terrible price as the government embraces a policy of export-led growth. Life of women workers in other zones is not very different and all the women employees in the four units have expressed apprehensions in revealing the actual conditions and spoke only after considerable persuasion and on condition of anonymity on many sensitive topics.

Smt. Rajyalakshmi gave an account of the status of women workers in SEZs in Noida which is as follows:

'*The women call it 'the Boundary'. The barbed-wire fence which encloses them for up to 12 hours a day lies hidden behind a facade of manicured lawns and smart-looking buildings of the Noida Export Processing Zone (NEPZ), 24 km from India's capital city*'.

'Inside, it is hot, dirty and dangerous. Security is tight - humiliating body-searches are routine - and trade union activity is forbidden. But for the nearly 4,000 women - many landless, illiterate and unskilled - who work in the zone, the choices are stark: work under these appalling conditions or starve'.

'She was six months pregnant. Her baby died in her stomach. It was blue, we learnt later. She was like any other worker who stood for eight or more hours,' an employee who requested anonymity says of a colleague'.

'I lied about my marital status at the time of recruitment,' adds another. 'We had to send our three-month-old baby to my parents' home as we cannot afford a private crèche'.

She also noted that 'Established in 1985, NEPZ is one of six such zones in the country. Women make up 40 per cent of its workforce. Like export processing zones (EPZs) across Asia, factories here like to hire women - preferably single - believing them to be more docile and productive than men. Between 1994 and 1996, the number of women workers here tripled while that of men doubled as India pursued an aggressive growth strategy'. Tales like these are common in almost all the zones. And there is a grave need to look into these aspects to better the lot of women workers.

The growth and profits of these trade zones increased but that brought little cheer to the lives of workers, especially women. In many of the units, wages are lower than outside and workers have to cope with harsh working and pitiful living conditions at workplace which lacks proper sanitation, clean water and access to government schools and health services. Full maternity benefits are not provided and minimum wages are not enforced, particularly in the case of women workers. And employers often avoid making provident fund and gratuity contributions and bonus payments.

Women workers lose their jobs once it is know that they are pregnant. And to avoid these women workers have frequent and unsafe abortions for fear of losing their jobs. But these are hushed up and don't come out into the open.

Respiratory problems, pelvic inflammatory disease and severe cases of dehydration are common. Anaemia among the women workers is chronic and severe. Miscarriages are not uncommon and are due to forced overtime, coupled with women's double burden of having to do housework as well.

Under these circumstances, it is important for the government to intervene and appoint regulatory bodies to overlook that basic and necessary facilities are provided to the women workers in these units. The importance of women's economic role is not reflected at the level of policy or practice in the zones, and most government agencies, investors, workers' organizations and other concerned groups should do more to ensure that the distinct concerns of women are addressed. Women workers' experience the living and working conditions differently from men and hence these matters deserve more attention and not just because the majority of zone workers are women. Any problem associated with zones has a more severe impact on the female workforce as women are generally in a weaker position than their male colleagues.

Women are traditionally responsible for social reproduction in most of the countries where these zones operate while men handle economic production. But of late, due to the changing attitudes, structural adjustment of the economy and poverty many women were forced on to the labour market. Though some of the women are the only major income earners in the household, this newfound status had not relieved them from their domestic responsibilities. This forces the women to wake up early to finish their household chores before they proceed to work and even after long hours of work, they have to come back and take care of the family members and prepare food for them. This extra burden adds to their fatigue and stress levels increase which may act as a distraction at work if the woman is worried about the health, well-being or security of family members. Another big concern for working women is child care which along with other domestic burdens may be the cause of late-coming, absenteeism and high labour turnover.

The work environment and conditions raise concerns for both men and women workers, especially for those at the lower end of the occupational and skill hierarchy but women tend to be worse off. Employers often complain of high labour turnover, low productivity, absenteeism and tardiness but these problems have their root causes in the unsatisfactory social and working conditions which many women face. There are many issues which need to be considered to improve the working conditions of female zone workers to create and cultivate a stable, long-term workforce which can produce world-class products.

Women workers often end up with stereotyped jobs at the lower end of the occupational hierarchy because of their perceived dexterity, small fingers or compliance and as a result the distribution of women in the workforce does not reflect their educational level. Though the zones increased women's access to jobs their education, which is often higher than the requirements for the job, or their experience, is not utilized properly and does not show in the productivity.

Even when similar functions are performed by both men and women, women tend to be paid at lower rates than men, because they generally occupy the lower-skill jobs. This clearly shows the sexual bias in the division of labour inside the units which discriminates against the women employees.

Though it is often assumed that the female worker provides only a secondary income to the household and will work for a shorter period of time than a male because of her reproductive role, this is frequently not the case in developing countries with a high proportion of female-headed households. Most of the women are also expected to care for the elderly or other members of the household and these responsibilities place severe burden on women's earnings, time and energy.

The long hours of work in EPZs poses a greater health and safety problem for women workers because of their additional domestic responsibilities and increased vulnerability to harassment or attack when traveling to or from work at odd hours and in the dark.

In all the units, welfare measures and social security provisions are virtually nil for the women zone workers. Women find it difficult to be economically independent without a pension or provident fund after leaving zone employment and without some training they are often unable to find alternative employment as many female zone workers perform only semi-skilled repetitive functions. This forces them to leave the zone without a craft or the life skills that would enable them to be gainfully employed elsewhere or to work independently after they leave the present job.

Female workers find it difficult to gain access to affordable and nutritious food and if they have to provide for their families the ramifications are more far-reaching. As a result of lack of proper food, women workers are often undernourished and are prone to illness.

There is a dearth of services dealing with family planning issues and sexually transmitted diseases in the communities surrounding the units. The social environment condemns unmarried mothers, leaving young women workers to deal with and hush up unwanted pregnancies. Given the sensitive nature of this problem, exact statistics on abortions are not readily available, but it has been established that in many zone communities a large number of illegal abortions are performed.

One of the important problems where hard data scarcely exists is sexual harassment. It is a sensitive topic and women workers do need protection against it. Though not much data is available, ILO missions received a disturbing number of indications that suggest the presence of harassment in the zones and it says it may even be widespread. Sexually harassed women have no independent and confidential office or service to turn to, and providing counselling services for women should be one of the major aspects which should be looked into by the zone administrators.

The third Chapter focused on the socio-economic problems of the women in the units. It is noted that the VSEZ mainly employs young unmarried women, most of them belonging to the Hindu religion and many from the backward community. The Study reveals that all the women workers of the zone are literate and it signifies the changing trend among the urban industrial working women. The family background of the respondents shows that the workers belong to nuclear families. The occupations of the heads of the households show that neither they are engaged in prestigious occupations nor minimal jobs. Half of the sampled workers play a major role in decision-making regarding family expenditure. But the Study amply proves that the women workers working in these units are having low socio-economic background.

It could be summarised that the women workers in the SEZ units in Visakhapatnam city are supporting their families bringing in almost half the family income. The determinants of income of the women workers were analysed with the help of multiple regressions. Education, age, marital status and experience could be considered as significant variables explaining income variations. The determinants of income may not be same across the four units of women workers in the present Study. The regression results relating to the WWD unit indicate that the coefficient of $\bar{R}^2$ is consistently positive in all the equations.

Is could thus be concluded that habits of the head of the household, absence of male head in families and social obligations seem to be obstructing the people in the VSEZ units to live above the poverty line, although they have 'entitlement' in terms of income.

The sixth Chapter which looked into the effects of migration revealed certain insights which are peculiar only to the units in our country. Skeldon argues that the movement of population can be a significant factor for the alleviation of poverty. In case of international migration, this may partly hold true but in the Indian context this cannot be an appropriate solution. The Study revealed that most of the workers continue to live in poor conditions despite the migration. However, it also depends on how one perceives poverty. In a narrow economic sense of low levels of income then migration may help in poverty eradication but in a broader perspective of human development which embraces better quality of life with access to basic necessities, migration cannot be considered as promoting human development. Migration is perceived by governments, policy-makers and urban planners in India as undesirable. The population living in the slum settlements in cities is showing an upward trend and the mushrooming growth of slum population exerts increased pressure on provision of minimum basic services such as housing, water supply, health, education and other basic infrastructure including sanitation. Supply of these services is one of the biggest challenges to all urban planners and policymakers.

In the VSEZ units, 69.45 per cent are migrant women and a majority of them belong to the same district (38.89 per cent). The proportion of migrants is significant from wage labourers followed by agricultural labourers, business and tailoring. The proportion of the migrants respondents migrated with their father/mother is highest at 45.83 per cent. All together 86 per cent of migrants have been residing in the city for less than 10 years. Migrant workers, on an average, are having more family income. A majority is living in thatched houses (43.73 per cent) and with regard to house ownership status; the migrant workers have no better status. These women workers belong to lower middle income group and there are no significant differences between local and migrant women workers with respect to socio-economic characteristics. There is neither legal protection for the migrant women working in the VSEZ units nor any job security. But they all face long hours of work, low wages and no basic facilities. The migrant women are working under bad sanitary and unsafe conditions.

The Study suggests that there is need for construction of concrete houses by the management to improve the living conditions of the workers in the VSEZ, otherwise, to provide house rent allowance as an incentive to the workers.

7.3 Suggestions and Policy Implications:

The Study suggests the following measures to improve the lot of the women workers in the VSEZ:

1. Though there is no provision for trade unions, women should form into some sort of self help groups or units to have a strong and united voice at least to demand for the basic facilities. The national trade union of the country should take effective steps to organize the workers.

2. Women workers should be protected from losing their jobs after child birth. Crèche and child care centres should be provided and counselors should be appointed to deal with the women's family and personal

problems. Full salary should be paid to women who take maternity leave.

3.Proper health facilities should be provided to women who suffer from long hours in standing posture and other health hazards faced due to dust pollution and other work related problems.

4. Workers should be educated about the hazards at the workplace and all of them should be given at least some basic training on safety. The Labour Ministry needs to play a decisive role during the formulation of polices in relation to women workers.

5. Women are a majority in the zone hence they need special attention. The Government should take steps to implementation of minimum wages.

6. Labour Commissioner and the factory inspectors should ensure that the units in the zone comply with the existing laws. The managements should also regularise the working hours and enhance the wage payments; especially the over-time wages and introduces night shift allowance.

7. Proper medical facilities should be provided along with regular check-ups for the women employees, many of whom seem to be undernourished and anemic. Clean drinking water, rest rooms, proper and hygienic toilets should be provided separately for women employees.

8. On the broader perspective, Government should intervene and appoint regulating authority to look into the complaints of sexual harassment, discrimination and other working conditions.

7.4 New Directions for Future Research

1. The present Study identified that there are hazards at workplaces and also brought to light the necessity of providing training on health and safety measures to women folk. These aspects call for further investigation to understand the reasons.

2. There is an uproar among the residents nearby the Zone that dumping of raw material, industrial affluents are polluting water and causing unhygienic surroundings with adverse effects on their health and well-being and also on habitat. These aspects call for further study by the experts on the environment/ecology.

Appendix -1.1
Area Particulars of the VSEZ

Particulars	Area (In Acres)
Area Developed	213.00
Area Under Developed	50.00
Area to be Developed	97.50
Total	360.50

Source: Data collected from the office of the VSEZ, Visakhapatnam.
As shown ante italics.

Appendix -1.2

Zonal Investment in the VSEZ from 1997-98 to 2003-04.

(Rs.in Crores)

Year	Government	Private	Total
1997-98	10.75	76.50	87.25
1998-99	7.50	65.75	73.25
1999-2k	6.30	58.25	64.55
2000-01	5.50	46.45	51.95
2001-02	4.45	26.60	31.05
2002-03	3.25	24.00	27.25
2003-04	1.55	14.03	15.50

Appendix -1.3

Exports of the VSEZ from 1997 to 2004.

Country	Exports (In Crores)	Percentage
Europe	1013.87	79.42
Gulf	100.90	7.90
U.S.A.	96.80	7.58
U.K.	41.38	3.24
Hong Kong	21.00	1.65
Australia	02.63	0.21
Total	1276.58	100.00

Appendix -1.4

Year -Wise Targets of the VSEZ.

Year	Targets (In Crores)	Reaching Targets (In Crores)
1997-98	---	----
1998-99	100.00	95.00
1999-2k	150.00	140.00
2000-01	200.00	219.00
2001-02	250.00	249.60
2002-03	400.00	357.57
2003-04	500.00	435.00
Total	1600.00	1495.57

Appendix -1.5

Developmental Expenditure of the VSEZ.

(Rs.Crores)

Year	Developmental Expenditure
1989-90	52.00
1990-91	149.12
1991-92	132.57
1992-93	229.00
1993-94	575.00
1994-95	435.03
1995-96	81.90
1996-97	150.00
1997-98	75.00
1998-99	---
1999-2k	400.00
2000-01	400.00
2001-02	637.00
2002-03	155.00
2003-04	37.75
Total	3509.37

Appendix - 1.6

Gender – Wise Distribution of Employees in Selected Units of the VSEZ

S. No	Name of the Establishment	Male	Female	Total
1	World-wide Diamond Industry	268 (48.91)	280 (51.09)	548
2	L.I.D. Jewelry	409 (50.25)	405 (49.75)	814
3	Madras knitting	103 (31.40)	225 (68.60)	328
4	Bangalore sweaters	55 (36.67)	95 (63.33)	150
	Total	835 (45.38)	1005 (54.62)	1840

Note: Figures in the parenthesis indicate percentages

Appendix -1.7

Unit -Wise Area, Registration and Stage of Implementation of the VSEZ

Sl.No.	Registration No. & Date	Name of the Unit	Area (In Squares)	Stage of Implementation
1	9/EPZ/21/1996	Coromandel expo-pack	2,500	Effecting deemed exports
2	9/EPZ/31/1997	Pooja Scrap Industry	4,500	Seasonal Industry
3	9/EPZ/29/1997	Seshi Agro Foods	1,600	Effecting Exports
4	9/EPZ/27/1997	World Wide Diamonds	4,500	Effecting Exports
5	EOB/216//1998	Bangalore Sweaters	750	Effecting Exports
6	9/EPZ/37/1998	Essem Informations	2,300	Effecting deemed exports
7	9/EPZ/40/1998	L.V. Fintrade	750	Effecting Exports
8	9/EPZ/49/1999	Gayathri Automobiles	820	Effecting Exports
9	9/EPZ/61/1999	Global Opticals	1000	Effecting Exports
10	9/EPZ/53/1999	Madras Knitwear	450	Effecting Exports
11	9/EPZ/59/1999	Net Decisions	1,500	Effecting Exports
12	9/EPZ/51/1999	Pyxis Technology	630	Effecting Exports
13	9/SEZ/64/2000	Cambridge Systems	630	Effecting Exports
14	9/EPZ/65/2000	Phoenix Cyber Tech	630	Effecting Exports
15	9/EPZ/79/2000	True Forge Fitting	1000	Effecting Exports
16	9/EPZ/86/2001	Ergo Bagen Fittings	10,000	Effecting Exports
17	9/SEZ/82/2001	Extreme IT Solutions	2,500	Effecting Exports
18	9/SEZ/81/2001	Xinth Technologies	1,500	Effecting Exports
19	9/EPZ/89/2002	L.I.D. Jewelry	630	Effecting Exports
20	9/SEZ/74/2004	Vanbueren Exports & Imports	3,200	Effecting Exports
	Total		41,390	

Appendix – 1.8
Establishment of Units and Women Workers in the VSEZ

S. No	Year of Establishment	Name of the Unit	Employees		Total
			Male	Female	
1	1996	Coromandel expo-pack	13 (100.00)	0	13
2	1997	Pooja Scrap Industry	31 (100.00)	0	31
3	1997	Seshi Agro Foods	7 (70.00)	3 (30.00)	10
4	1997	World Wide Diamonds	268 (48.91)	280 (51.09)	548
5	1998	Bangalore Sweaters	55 (36.67)	95 (63.33)	150
6	1998	Essem Informations	15 (75.00)	5 (25.00)	20
7	1998	L.V. Fintrade	9 (81.82)	2 (18.18)	11
8	1999	Gayathri Automobiles	135 (93.10)	10 (6.90)	145
9	1999	Global Opticals	10 (66.67)	5 33.33)	15
10	1999	Madras Knitwear	103 31.40)	225 68.60)	328
11	1999	Net Decisions	400 (90.91)	40 (9.09)	440
12	1999	Pyxis Technology	48 (82.76)	10 (17.24)	58
13	2000	Cambridge Systems	55 (84.62)	10 (15.38)	65
14	2000	Phoenix Cyber Tech	15 (60.00)	10 (40.00)	25
15	2000	True Forze Fitting	2 (100.00)	0	2
16	2001	Ergo Bagen Fittings	5 (100.00)	0	5
17	2001	Extreme IT Solutions	14 (87.50)	2 12.50)	16
18	2001	Xinth Technologies	35 (77.78)	10 (22.22)	45
19	2002	L.I.D. Jewelry	409 (50.25)	405 (49.75)	814
20	2004	Vanburen Exports & Imports	2 (100.00)	0	2
	Total		1586 (59.33)	1087 (40.67)	2673

Note: Figures in the parenthesis indicate percent

Appendix – 1.9
Year -Wise Zone Exports of the VSEZ

Year	Exports(In Crores)
1996-97	---
1997-98	0.04
1998-99	9.21
1999-0k	68.22
2000-01	149.97
2001-02	192.56
2002-03	361.89
2003-04	478.12
Total	1260.01

Appendix – 1.10
Year-Wise Break – up of Ownership Status

Year	Domestic	Foreign	Joint	Total
1996-97	01	--	--	01
1997-98	02	01	--	03
1998-99	02	01	--	03
1999-0k	03	02	--	05
2000-01	03	--	--	03
2001-02	01	--	--	01
2002-03	01	--	02	03
2003-004	--	--	01	01
Total	13	04	03	20

Appendix - 1.11
Unit – Wise Production Objectives of the VSEZ

Sl.No.	Registration No. & Date	Name of the Unit	Production Objectives
1	9/EPZ/21/1996	Coromandel expo-pack	Corrugated Packing Materials
2	9/EPZ/31/1997	Pooja Scrap Industry	Recycling of imported ferrous and non- ferrous scrap
3	9/EPZ/29/1997	Seshi Agro Foods	Mango, pulp and juices
4	9/EPZ/27/1997	World Wide Diamonds	Polishing of rough Diamonds
5	EOB/216//1998	Bangalore Sweaters	To produce Knitted garments
6	9/EPZ/37/1998	Essem Informations	Software Development
7	9/EPZ/40/1998	L.V. Fintrade	Plastic hub caps
8	9/EPZ/49/1999	Gayathri Automobiles	Polishing wheels, manufacturing of polishing consumables
9	9/EPZ/61/1999	Global Opticals	Ophthalmic lenses prepared
10	9/EPZ/53/1999	Madras Knitwear	To produce Knitted garments
11	9/EPZ/59/1999	Net Decisions	Software Development
12	9/EPZ/51/1999	Pyxis Technology	Software Development
13	9/SEZ/64/2000	Cambridge Systems	IT enabled services
14	9/EPZ/65/2000	Phoenix Cyber Tech	Software Development
15	9/EPZ/79/2000	True Forge Fitting	Recycling of Ferrous and non-ferrous scrap
16	9/EPZ/86/2001	Ergo Bagen Fittings	Tubular components by forging/forming
17	9/SEZ/82/2001	Extreme IT Solutions	Software Development
18	9/SEZ/81/2001	Xinth Technologies	Software Development
19	9/EPZ/89/2002	L.I.D. Jewelry	Diamond processing and to increase base and product
20	9/SEZ/74/2004	Vanbueren Exports & Imports	Railings and decorative product and trading.

ANNEXURE -1

ANDHRA UNIVERSITY, DEPARTMENT OF ECONOMICS
Schedule for the collection of data on
'Socioeconomic and working profile of women employed in the VSEZ'
(Visakhapatnam Special Economic Zone)

Name of the Respondent:	Designation:	Name of the establishment in VSEZ:
Age / (Date of Birth):	Education:	Marital status:
Mother tongue:	Other languages known:	Nationality:
Social Community:	Religion:	Any other subsidiary occupation:

A. Family Size:

S. No.	Name of the member	Relationship with the respondent	Sex	Age	Education	Occupation	Dependency	Income per month	Specific Remarks
1									
2									
3									
4									
5									
6									
7									

B.Employment/Income:

S.No	Questions	Answers
1	Since how long you are working in this establishment?	
2	Have you worked elsewhere in similar establishment? If so, give address:	
3	What was your earning in that establishment?	
4	Why you have left that establishment? Specify reasons:	
5	What type of work you do here?	
6	What type of skills you possess for this work?	

7	What type of equipment you use for the assigned work?	
8	How many hours you work for day? Specify the timings:	
9	Do you work for overtime? Mention the rate of work per hour:	Rs.
10	What is your income per month for this job/work?	Rs.
11	Are you happy with the working process?	Yes/No
12	If No, specify the reasons:	
13	Suggest how you want it to be (the work):	
14	How many leaves/types of leaves you are eligible per annum?	
15	Is the organosation extends maternity leave facility?	
16	Are you a member of any trade union? If so, name of the Union:	
17	Any other Pertinent question (not covered):	

C.Working Environment:

S.No	Cadre	The type of treatment				
		Friendly	Authoritatively	Abusively	With harassment	Others, if any specify
1	Executives					
2	Supervisors					
3	Colleagues					
4	Union Leaders					
5	Others, if any specify					

D. Infrastructure facilities:

S.No	Facilities	Conditions (light, ventilation, acoustic, etc)				Suggestions for improvement	Remarks (after your physical verification)
		Good	Satisf-actory	Bad	No		
1	Working Room/Office						
2	Drinking Water						
3	Dining Room						
4	Rest Room						
5	Toilets						
6	Crèche						
7	Others. specify						

E. Income, expenditure and savings:

S.No	Source	Opinion
1	Income from other than the present employment (like rents, subsidiary occupation, agriculture ect. Per annum in Rs):	
2	Income of the head of household (in Rs. per annum):	
3	Income from other earners in your family (in Rs. per annum):	
4	Total family income from all sources (in Rs.):	
5	Expenditure on food (in Rs. per annum):	
6	Expenditure on non- food items (in Rs. per annum):	
7	What is your savings (gold/ silver/cash etc worth in Rs.)?	
8	What are your liabilities (indebtedness in Rs.)?	
9	What are your investments (shares/certificates/bonds etc in Rs.)?	

F. Health:

S.No	Health status	Opinion
1	Prior to joining the VSEZ what your health status?	Good/Bad/As it is today/others, specify:
2	Do you have any health insurance or such other insurance policies? If so, specify:	
3	What type of health ailments often you suffer?	
4	Where do you get treatment for these ailments? (Specify mention may be made of health/medical facilities extended by (VSEZ)	
5	Do you consider this/these health ailment(s) is due to your working environment at VSEZ? If specify reasons:	
6	What type of measures you suggest to be of important for the working women in VSEZ?	

G. Migration:

S.No	Family members by relationship	Place of Birth/Nativity			Year of Migration/No of years
		Village name/Distance of VSPM in km	Mandal	District & State	
1	Self(informant)				
2	Father				
3	Mother				
4	Husband				
5	Brother				
6	Sister				
7	Others, specify the relationship:				

S.No	Reasons	Opinion
1	Who brought you to Visakhapatnam City?	
2	Who initiated to migrate?	
3	Why you have migrated?	
4	What was your employment when you are in your native place?	
5	Who supported you immediately after your arrival to Viskhaptnam?	
6	After your arrival how much time you spent to secure employment?	
7	How often you go to your native place?	
8	What items you get from your native place (domestic commodities)?	
9	How much money you send to your kith & kin in your native place?	
10	Are you satisfied with your city life?	
11	If yes, what are the reasons?	
12	If no, what are the reasons?	
13	If a similar employment is offered at your native place, would you like to go back?	
14	If yes, why?	
15	If no, why?	
16	How many months you stay in Visakhapatnam in a year?	
17	Any other, specify:	

H. Descriptive information on the problems and suggestions of the informants:

(Not covered in the schedule & use separate sheet for case study):

Signature of the Investigator with Date

ANNEXURE - 2

Historical Background of Visakhapatnam

Visakhapatnam, the port city is the jewel on the east coast of India. The City is a harmonious blend of magical past and the bustling present with a brief taking panorama of golden beaches, lush green fields, verdant valleys and splendid monuments from rich historical and religious heritage.

Matchless in beauty and landscape, Visakhapatnam is said to have derived its name from the deity "Viskha" (the God of Valour). The history of the town can be traced back to Asokha the Greate (272-232 B.C) when this was a small fishing village of the Kalinga Empire. Later on this port town successively passed from the Andhra Kings of Vengi to the Pallavas, Cholas and the Gangas and then later in the 15th Century Visakhapatnam became a part of the Vijaya Nagar Empire. The British took change of this beautiful land and transformed this town in to a busy and flourishing port town.

Visakhapatnam has always been an important location on the map of the country, right from the ancient times, especially during the British Rule. The city was the target of the anvying Japanese during Worl War II. The Pakistanis attacked the city during the Indo pak war in 1972, fortunately there was no damage to the city. Visakhapatnam is the head quarts of the eastern navel command of the Indian Navy.

The city is also experiencing a boom in tourism, as the city is and owed with un polluted beautiful beaches, stunning scenic landscape, rich cultural heritage and it has tremendous business potential. The three majestic rocky ranges- the Kailash Hill, the Porupalam Hill and the

Yarada Hill from an excellent backdrop and enhances the charm of this beautiful port city. As one enters the harbour, the three magnificent hills instantly catch our attention as they exbit the secular flavour of the town. Each one of them is adorned with a place of worship. A Roman Catholic Church perches atop the Kanyamarykonda (Ross Hill), The Durga Konda as a shrine of a Muslim Saint Ishaque Madina, while a temple nestles over the Venkateswera konda.

Visakhapatnam, the industrial hub has a lot to its credit. If it were not for the port of Visakhapatnam which was opened way back in the October of 1933, Visakhapatnam would still be a sleepy fishing village. The port of Visakhapatnam handles about 35.65 MT of cargo this year. This happens to be the maximum amount handle in the country. Now this port promises to become one of Asia's major ports by the 21st century.

- The opening of the shipyard in the early 40's by Seth Walachand Hirachand laid the early foundation for industrialization in Visakhapatnam. This later became nationalised and renamed as Hindustan Shipyard Limited.

- Next we have the opening of the 60,000 tpa oil refinery by caltex. This too was nationalised and renamed as Hindustan Petro Chemical Limited. HPCL now operates a 4.5 mtpa refinery.

- Wholly Government owned Bharat Heavy Plates and Vessels (BHPL) and enjoyed a sunny harvest during its inception in the early 70's and 80's, but later lost out to more eagar and competitive rivals like Larsen Toubro, Tata ect.

- By far and large the biggest industial investment in Visakhapatnam is the Rs. 8529 crore Steel Plants which became operational in 1981, though the foundation stone was laid in 1971.
    - The Export Processing Zones have a good infrastructure for software exporters.
    - Other important industries include

- Hindustan Zinc
- Visakha oil refinery
- Port Trust
- Coramandel Fertilisers
- LG Polymers
- Dredging Corporation of India
    - Power Projects
- "Navaratna" National Thermal Power Corporation-with a 1000 MW plant
- Hindujas with a 1040 Thermal Plant

- Simhadri Thermal Power Project is well under way

- Another Hinduja Project is to start later this year.

The State Government is doing quite a lot to make Andhra Pradesh into a mega Industrial Park. The A.P Industrial Infrastructure Corporation is in the process of developing the Visakhapatnam - Kakinada belt into a mega infrastructure and has acquired more than half of 8664 acres for this.

But top class infrastructure in Transport, Telecommunications and Tourist amenities are needed before the mega bucks start coming in to set up a base here.

ANNEXURE - 3

Annexure to G.O. Ms.No. 151, Inds & Comm. (IF) Department Dated 9-4-2002

Andhra Pradesh Special Economic Zone Policy

1. Preamble:

1.1 The Government of India has introduced the Special Economic Zones (SEZs) guidelines vide a revision in the Export-Import Framework 1997-2002

1.2 SEZs are specifically delineated enclaves treated as foreign territory for the purpose of industrial service and trade operation, with relaxation in customs duties and a more liberal regime in respect of other levies, foreign investments and other transactions. Domestic restrictions and infrastructure inadequacies would be removed in the SEZs to create an internationally benchmarked environment for business transactions and operations. Government of India guidelines suggests that SEZs can be developed in the public-private or joint sector domains, or by State Governments.

1.3 Special Economic Zone(s) development will primarily be led by Private Sector investors and Developers to undertake international class and scale infrastructure developments. These developers (herein after referred to as SEZ Company) will act as SEZ Managers in Designing, Planning, Financing, Building, Operating and Marketing the zones to investors. The SEZ Company would endeavor to provide world-class utilities, social and municipal services.

1.4 Government will facilitate creation of linkage and social infrastructure including telecom facilities, inter modal transport linkages (road, rail and air connectivity)

1.5 Andhra Pradesh Government intends to exploit the SEZ concept for impacting the State's socio-economic fabric through enhanced job opportunities and industrial development. Andhra Pradesh Industrial Infrastructure Corporation, APIIC Ltd. has already taken the lead in developing the SEZ at Achutapuram and Rambilli Mandals. Visakhapatanam Dist. As a public-private partnership.

1.6 APIIC is the nodal agency for the state of Andhra Pradesh for AP Special Economic Zones being developed at Atchutapuram and for other future SEZ developments in the State. APIIC will also perform as Interim Development Commissioner for the SEZs.

1.7 Development Commissioner: shall be deemed to be appropriate Development Authority for the notified area of SEZ.

1.8 With the background of GoI guidelines for SEZs, the State has decided to formulate the following SEZ Policy to provide a comprehensive framework for establishment, operations and sustainability of the Special Economic Zones in the State.

1.9 This Policy will have overbearing powers existing state policies on above issues. For issues and areas not covered by the SEZ Framework, the prevailing State Framework & legislation will be deemed to be in force.

Policy Framework:

2. Industries Department

2.1 Single Window Clearance: The Special Economic Zone will provide for a single Window Clearance for approvals and clearances for investors. This will be targeted for timely clearances using electronic formats on Electronic Data Interchange (EDI) platform.

a. Each Special Economic Zone will designate a Development Commissioner (DC). DC would be the Designated Authority representing State and Central Government and their agencies for all investments by SEZ Units for the Specific SEZ.

b. Single window for all agencies of Government of Andhra Pradesh including Power, water, Commercial Tax Department (sales tax, entertainment tax), Food & Drug Administration, Andhra Pradesh Pollution Control Board (APPCB), Industries & Commerce Department, Commissioner of Industries/District Industries Commissioner, Chief Inspector of Factories, State Labour Officer, Employment Exchange Officer (Apprenticeship Act etc.) District Fire Officer, AP Transco, Police Department (Foreigners' registration cell) available at SEZ etc. and other terms and agencies included from time to time by GoAP,

Officials of above state departments and agencies will be nominated to DC's office to assist the DC on a need basis, at the discretion of the DC.

2.2 Simplified Business Working Environment: All procedures will have pre-laid guidelines and time lines for disposing off cases as well as approval with certification fees.

a. Self-certification will be enabled for all industries using empanelled private sector inspection agencies.

b. To the extent possible, regulation and governance on the SEZ shall rest with the DC. Physical inspections would be undertaken in accordance with schedule in consultation with DC.

c. Exemption for small scale industries and IT industries from registration.

d. SEZ Company will provide necessary infrastructure (building, office space and equipment) for DC and pay equitable amounts as salary and prerequisites to the DC's office staff through suitable escrow account.

2.3 Development Authority:

a) The Development Commissioner is deemed to be appropriate authority for the Industrial Development Area for the notified SEZ area.

b) Role of Development Commissioner

Regulation: To provide clearances under various statues and regulations of Government of India and State Government.

Facilitation: To facilitate clearances not granted within the SEZ and advice Government on issues requiring Framework amendments of clarifications.

Promotion: To undertake marketing of the zones along with private promoter.

3. Revenue Department :

3.1 50 per cent exemption will be allowed on Stamp Duty, Registration Fee on transfer of lands meant for Industrial use in the Special Economic Zone area.

3.2 Complete exemption of stamp duty and registration fee for loan agreements, credit deeds, mortgages and hypothecation deeds executed by the SEZ Units for assets in the SEZ in favour of banks or financial institutions will also be allowed.

3.3 With due regard to the National Uniform floor rate policy and exemptions given to SEZs throughout the Country, the State Government proposes to extend the following exemptions to AP-SEZ, Achutapuram.

'Other state taxes including sales tax, VAT, luxury tax and entertainment tax and state duties on transactions within SEZ. Sale tax and other State Taxes on inputs (goods and services) made to SEZ units from Off Zone suppliers within the State.

A Consensus would also be attempted at National level for exemption being given to SEZs throughout the country.

4. Energy Department :

4.1 The State exempts Power in SEZ from Electricity Duty and Tax.

4.2 Captive Power will be allowed in SEZ. Government will take a view as to whether SEZ units will be given exemption from wheeling charges and grid protection charges levied on Captive Power.

4.3 The APSEZ will take necessary steps to make arrangements in respect of transmission, distribution and collection of bills"

5. Water Supply:

The SEZ Company will ensure the provision of adequate water supply within the SEZ.

6. Labour Department :

6.1 The State Govt. delegates power of Labour Commissioner to the DC.

6.2 State Govt. will also place an officer of Labour Department under the DC.

6.3 The State Govt. approves simplified submissions of reports by SEZ Units and created a Consolidated Annual Report System. Self-Certification is also approved.

6.4 Appropriate officials with DC will be designated as Inspectors, Conciliation Officers and Registration Officers under the labor laws to provide Single Window service.

6.5 For inspection relating to workers' health and safety, the State Government permits units to undertake inspection by accredited agencies notified by DC.

6.6 Summary of proposed simplifications under labour laws is given at Appendix-A.

7. Environment Department and Andhra Pradesh Pollution Contro Board:

7.1 Development Commissioner will be notified as the appropriate authority to represent the APPCD, with regard to clearances for all SEZ Units. In respect of inspections pertaining to pollution control, these would be taken up by the Pollution Control Staff deputed to the Development Commissioner of SEZ.

7.2 SEZ does not require Environment Impact Assessment (EIA) approval.

7.3 Industrial Approvals:

7.3 (a) Non-Polluting Units: Approval will be based on SEZ EIA Master Plan. DC will provide Consent for Establishment and Operations.

7.3 (b) Polluting Units: SEZ Level Empowered Committee (with experts nominated by MOEF, APPCBO will assist DC in speedy approvals to polluting units. Such Units will approach Ministry of Environment and Forests, GoI and receive consent on EIA within 45 days.

7.4 Operating Framework for Industries:

a. Periodic Self Certification for all industries in the SEZ assisted by private certification agencies. Random sampling monitoring by DC of Units for environmental management.

b. Afforestation: SEZ Level Empowered Committee may grant approvals for developments on specific pockets based on compensatory afforestation in line with guidelines established by SEZ Town Planning Authority.

c. No Development Zone: Government will consider establishing a no industrial development zone around the SEZ periphery, to extent possible as a green belt in order to avoid unplanned development.

8. Municipal Administration Department and Panchayat Raj Department :

8.1 The State Government will declare the SEZ as a local authority, which shall replace the existing Panchayats. Such local authority will be vested with all powers and shall carry out all functions in the existing provisions. The State Government may further declare this local authority as a Municipality.

8.2 SEZ land will be notified in line with the SEZ Master plan approved by DC. The SEZ Master Plan will be undertaken in accordance with international best practice in town planning and Environment and Social Management Planning norms. Town planning Authority (with nominees from State and SEZ Company) will be established for regulating land usage in SEZ.

9. Home Department :

The State govt. will process creation of State Police, Fire Services and Home Guard Structures for SEZ(s) for the maintenance of Law & Order.

10. Law Department :

Special territorial jurisdiction will be accorded to Special Courts as necessary in the SEZ, in consonance with High Court approvals. Prescribed court fee and suitable service fees may be notified for such courts.

11. Education Framework :

The State Gov. will facilitate development and augmentation of education and training facilities through suitable formats including private sector formats. The education policy for SEZ aims to proactively create highly skilled and managerial human resource bases in line with the needs and dynamics of international markets.

12. All other Policies of the State would remain in force for the SEZ, unless they a amended by the appropriate authority.

ANNEXURE – 4

Labour Framework for SEZ Amendments to

1. Industries Disputes Act, 1947.

Notified 100% EUs as Public Utility Services Exemption from Sec 9A-Notice of Charge to SEZ Units Development Commissioner delegated powers for Sec 25-M and 25-N Development Commissioner and other senior officers notified as Conciliation Officers for SEZ. Deletion in Chapter V.B (2 months advance period for Lay offs/ retrenchment) from Act.

Top

2. Minimum Wages Act, 1948:

a) Exemptions under Sec 18, 11 and 13 Sec 18 - Maintenance of Registers and Records. Sec 13-Fixing hours for normal work days.

b) Jurisdictional Labour Officer to be notified as Inspector under Minimum Wages Act., Payment of Bonus Act and Payment of Gratuity Act.

Simplification of Procedures: Changes by notification

3. AP Shops and Establishments Act, 1988

Top

Suitable exemptions to make possible 365 days working for 24 hours in a day, provided suitable overtime allowance is paid.

Top

4. Industrial Employment (Standing Orders) Act, 1946

Exemption from publication of working time, wage rate and shift working

Top

5. Contract Labour Employment

Power of registering and licensing delegated to jurisdictional Labour Officer

Sec. 31 presently allows exemption by State under emergency -

amendment to empower appropriate Govt. to exempt establishments from Act without reference to Emergency.

Top

6. Payment of Equal Remuneration, 1976:

Appointment of two State Officers to SEZ-DC to be designated as Authority and nominee to SEZ as Inspector for SEZ.

Top

7. Trade Union Act, 1926

Exclude outsiders from becoming officer bearers of a Trade Union. The Govt. has agreed that at least 30 per cent of workmen employed be members of the recognized Trade Union.

8. Single Labour Authority

Factories Act, 1948 - issuing notification of labour officer in SEZ as Inspector and Chief Inspector of Factories for units in SEZ.

9. General Provisions

Introducing a provision in Factories Act for exempting Units located in an SEZ area or of a class of units from all or some provisions of the Act. Enabling Chief Inspector of Factories to give approvals within 15 days for approval of plans, canteen and registration of Factories.

JAINDER SINGH
PRINCIPAL SECRETARY TO GOVERNMENT &
COMMISSIONER FOR INDUSTRIAL PROMOTION

SELECT BIBLIOGRAPHY

Afhar, H. (1992) : *Women and Adjustment Policies*. London.

Ahmed, Karuna (1979) : "Studies of Educated Working Women in India-Trends issues", *Economic and Political Weekly*, Vol.XIV, No.33. August.

Alam, K. (1987) : *The changing role of women in the rural Economic of Asia*. Conference volume of the Indian Economic Association Seventh Annual Conference, Jaipur.

Andall, Jacqueline (2000) : *Gender, Migration and Domestic Service*, Ashgate, US.

Annabel, Rodda (1991) : "Women and the Environment", Zed Books Ltd., London & New Jersey.

Ashok Kundra (2000) : *The Performance of India's Export Zones*, Sage Publications, New Delhi.

Ashok Mitra (1951) : Censes *of India*, volume. West Bengal, part-1.

----------------(1951) : *The status of women, Literacy and employment*. ICSSR, Allied Publisher.

Bandyopadhyay (1995) : "Hunger and Jobless Growth"-Impact of SAP. *Manistream*, May13.

Beena (1991) : "Technological changes and women workers: The case of Fish Processing Industry in Kerala", in Chetana Kalbagh (ed), Women and Development, Vol.1, Discovery Publishing House, New Delhi.

Bhagya Lakshmi, J. (2005) : "Towards Equality at work" *Kurukshetra*, May, Vol. 53, No.9.

Bogchi, J. (1976) : "Killed with Kindness", *Economic and Political Weekly*, 24th January.

Boseup, Ester (1970) : *Women's Role in Economic development*, St Martin Press, New York.

Burggrat, S.P.U.(1984) : "Women, Youth and Minorities and Case of missing Productivity", *American Economic Review*, May.

Carbo, V. and Steloner (1983) : "Earnings Determination and Labour Market", *Journal of Development Economics*, Vol. 12.

Centre for Women's Development Studies (1997) : *Sites of Struggle*, Case study of women workers in Noida, 1997-98.

Chandrasekhar Rao, D. (2004) : "Changing trends in Work Participation rates and Women Employment in India", Paper presented at National Seminar, 30th & 31st December, Department of Economics, Andhra University, Visakhapatnam.

Dastur (1960) : *A Doctor's Approach to Industrial Medicine*, Tata Institute of Social Sciences, Mumbai.

Desai, K.G. (1969) : "A Study of Workers' Expectations from Supervisors and Management", *the Indian Journal of Social Work*, Vol. XXX, No.2, July.

Desai, Neera (1987) : *Women and Society in India*, Ajantha Publications, New Delhi.

Divya & Pandey (1993) : *Migrant Labour and Gender Dimension-Micro Analysis of Gender Differentials in Migrant Workers*, Research Centre for Women's Studies. S.N.D.T. Women' University, Mumbai.

Duraiswamy, P.M. (1997) : "Gender Bias in the Scientific and Technical Labour Markets: A Comparative Study of Tamil Nadu and Kerala," Centre for Development Studies, Trivandrum.

Durganand Sinha (1998) : "Job Satisfaction in Office and Manual Workers," *the Indian Journal of Social Work*. Vol.XIX. No. 1, June.

Elson, D. (1981) : *The Subordination of Women and the Internationalisation of Factory Production*, Routledge. London.

Everetts Lee (1975) : *Theory of Migration*, Kenneth, U.K. Kamneyer (ed.,).

Ganguli, B.N. (1973) : *Population and Development*, S. Chand & Co. Pvt. Ltd., New Delhi.

Gayatri (2002) : *Gender, Poverty and Employment in India*, unpublished Paper, ILO, New Delhi.

Ghosh Balasnisikha (1984) : "Displacement of the Female in the Indian Labour Force", *Economic and Political Weekly*.

Godgil, D.R. (1965) : *Women in the working force in India, Kunde data Memorial lecture*, Asian Publishing House. New Delhi.

Government of India (1969) : *Report of the National Commission on Labour*, Ministry of Labour, New Delhi.

Government of India (1974) : *Towards Equality: Report of the Committee on the Status of women in India,* New Delhi, Department of Social Welfare.

Government of India (1988) : *Department of Rural Development*, Ministry of Agriculture: Annual Report-1987-88.

Government of India, (1997) : *Annual Report 1997-98*, Ministry of Commerce, New Delhi.

Government of India (2000) : *National Sample Survey Consumption Expenditure Data (55th Round, 1999-2000)*, Planning Commission, New Delhi.

Government of India (2001) : *Census Report 2001*, New Delhi.

Government of India (2001) : *Planning Commission Report*, Ministry of Finance.

Government of India (2003) : *The Ministry of Labour and Employment*, New Delhi.

Government of India (2003) : Economic Survey 2003-04, New Delhi.

Griffen, K. (1974) : *Land Concentration and Rural Poverty*, London, McMillan.

Gupta, O.P. (1972) : "Volume, Factors and Characteristics of Migration to Urban Delhi", *Indian Census Centenary Seminar,* Vol.1, Office of the Registrar-General of India. Ministry of Home Affairs, New Delhi.

Gupta, S.P. (Ed) (1996) : *China's Economic Reforms: The role of Special Economic Zones and Economic and technological development zones*, Allied Publishers Ltd., New Delhi.

I.L.O. (1958) : "Employment and Occupation", Geneva.

I.L.O. (2003) : *Women in Changing World*, Geneva.

ICFTU (1998) : "Behind the wire: Anti union repression in the EPZs", this information is present on the website of *ICFTU* under the heading EPZs.

ILO (1998) : *Labour and Social Issues relating to Export Processing Zones.*

ILO / UNCTC (1988) : *Economic and Social Effects of Multinational Enterprises in Export Processing Zones*, Geneva. ILO.

ILO/UNCTC (1988) : *Economic and Social Effects of Multinational Enterprises in Export Processing Zones*, Geneva: ILO.

Indrani Majumdar (2001) : "EPZs and their workers in India: A Study of the Noida Export Processing Zone" Ed in *Labour issues in Export Processing Zones in South Asia: Role of Social Dialogue* by A.S. Oberai, A. Sivananthiran and C.S. Venkata Ratnam.

International Labour Organisation (1982) : *Rural Department and Women in Asia.*

International Labour Organisation (1972) : "Employment, Income and Equity, A Strategy for Increasing Productive Unemployment in Kenya", Geneva.

Ismail Hossain (2001) : *Export Processing Zones in Bangladesh and industrial relations*, Ed. by A.S. Oberoi & Others.

Jagadish Prasad (1987) : Women in the labourforce: a case study of Bihar, conference volume of the Indian Economic Association, Seventh Annual Conference, Jaipur.

Jayanti (1987) : *Role of women in Urban Development. A case study of Tirupati Town*, (Unpublished dissertation), Department of Economics, S.V.University, March.

Jocobson, J.L. (1993) : "Women's Health: the price of poverty", in Koblinsky, M., Timyan, J. and Gay, J. (ed.,), *The Health of Women: A Global Perspective*, Boulder Colorado, West View Press.

John Connel and Biplab Das Gupta (1976) : *Migration from Rural Areas*, Oxford University Press, Delhi.

John Zechariah (1983) : "Employer's Expectation from a Supervisor", *The Indian Journal of Social Work*, XLIV, No.3, October.

Kapur, P. (1970) : "*Marriage and Working Women in India*", Delhi

Kenneth Kamneyer (1975) : *Population Studies Selected Essays and Research*, Chicago.

Kingsley Danis (1950) : *The Population of India and Pakistan*, Princeton, New Jersey.

Kumar R (1990) : "Health of Working Women", in Ram Kumar (Ed), *Women, Health, Development and administration: Principles and Practice*, Vol. 1, Deep and Deep Publications, New Delhi.

Kumar Rajiv (1982) : *India's export processing zones*. Oxford University Press, India.

Lalitha Devi (1902) : *Status and Employment of Women on India*. B.R. Publishing Corporation, Delhi.

Lalitha Iyer (1990) : "Overview of Employment in the Food and Drink Industries", in Divys Pandey & Mira Savara (ed). '*Between the Farm and Thali-Women and Food Processing*, Research Centre for Women Studies, S.N.D.T., Womens University, Mumbai.

Lalitha Iyer (1990A) : "Overview of Employment in the Food and Drink Industries" in Divya Pandey & Mira Savara (ed). *Between the Farm and Thali-Women and Food Processing*, Research Centre for Women's Studies, S.N.D.T. Women's University, Bombay.

Lee, Eddy (Ed) (1984) : *Export Processing Zones and Industrial Employment in Asia*, Bangkok: ILO-ARTEP.

M.Viswanadhan, (1994) : *Women in Agriculture and Rural development*, Print well, Jaipur, Rajasthan.

Madhavi.A.D and Vijayalakshmi. M. (2001) : "Freedom of Association and Promotion of Social Dialogue in EPZs of India", Ed in *Labour issues in Export Processing Zones in South Asia: Role of Social Dialogue* by A.S. Oberai, A. Sivananthiran and C.S. Venkata Ratnam.

Maex, Rudy (1983) : *Employment and Multinationals in Asian Export Processing Zones*, ILO, Geneva.

Mahajan, A. (1966) : "Women's Two Roles: a case study of Role Conflict." *Indian Journal of Social Work*, 24 (4).

Manjudar, T. (1977) : "The urban poor and social change: A case study of squatter settlements in Delhi", *Social Action* 27(3).

Mathew (1991A) : " Exploitation of Women Labour Employment in Kerala." in Chetan Kalbagh (ed). Women and Development, Vol. 2, Discovery Publishing House, New Delhi.

Mathew (1991B) : "Women and the so-called Informal Sector-Strategies and Counter Strategies", in Chetana Kalbagh (ed), *Women and Development*, Vol. 5, Discovery Publishing House, New Delhi.

Mazumdar, D. and Ahmad, M. (1978) : "Labour Market segmentation and determination of earnings", *World Bank Staff Working Paper*, No. 278, Washington.

Mazumdar, D.N. (1960) : *Social Contours of an Industrial City*, Asia Publishing House, Bombay.

Mazumdar, T. (1979) : "Paradigms in the study of urban Markets in LDC's – A measurement in the light of an empirical survey in Bambay city", *World Bank Staff Working Paper*, No.366, Washington D.C.

Mincer, J. (1974) : *Schooling, Experience and earning*, NBER, New York.

Mishra, Sridar, (1952) : "Urban Employment and Migration of Agriculture Labour in U.P." *Rural India*, 15 (3), March.

Mohan, R. (1981) : "The Determinants and Labour Earnings in Developing Metropolies- Estimates from Bagota", Kali Colombia, *World Bank Staff Working Paper*, No.498, Washington D.C.

Murty, K.S. (1986) : "Urbain Labour Informal Sector-A Case Study of Visakhapatnam City", B.R.P.C., Delhi.

Nasreen, Fazalbhoy (1988) : *The Health Status of Indian Women*, Unit for Urban Studies, T.I.S.S., Mumbai.

Nath Kamal (1968) : "Women in the working force in India", *Economic and Political Weekly*, August.

Neera, Desai (1990A) : "Women Food Processors- Work without Reward", in Divya Pandey & Mira Savara (ed), *Between the Farm and Thali-Women and Food Processing*, Research Centre for Women's Studies, S.N.D.T. Women's University, Bombay.

Neeta Anand (2003) : "Working Women: Issues and Problems" *Yojana*, March.

Nirmala, B. (1991) : "The more it changes, the more it is the same- Women Workers in Export Oriented Industries", in Nirmala Benerjee (ed), *Indian Women in a Changing Industrial Scenario*, Sage Publications, New Delhi.

Nirmala, Banerjee (1991) : "The more it changes, the more it is the same- Women workers in Export Oriented Industries". in Nirmala Banerjee (ed), *Indian Women in a Changing Industrial Scenario*, Sage Publications, New Delhi.

Park, K. (1995) : *Park's Text book of Preventive and Social Medicine*, 14th edition, Banarsidas Bhanot Publishers, Jabalpur, India.

Patel, G. Harbhai (1987) : "Kerala Migrant Female Labour in Fishing units of Viraval City of Western India" in Vidyut Joshi (Ed) *Migrant Labour abd Related Issues*, Oxford & IBH Publishing Co. Pvt. Ltd., Gandhi Labour Institute, Ahmadabad.

Peterson, William (1958) : "A General Typology of Migration", *American Studies Review*, Vol.23, June.

Planning Commission (1978) : *Working group on women 1978*, New Delhi.

Prabhakar, R. (1975) : *Study of Hundred – Employed Women in Udaypur*, University of Delhi (Thesis Unpublished).

Radha Devi, D. and Ravinder, D. (1985) : "Working women and household work", *Social Change*, Vol. 15. No.2.June.

Rajiv Kumar (1998) : *India's Export Processing Zones.*

Rama Devi K.(2003) : AIDWA *'Praja Sakthi'* Visakhapatnam, July. 2003

Rama Prabha (2003) : *CITU, VSEZ: EPZs and globalization past experience and future challenges*, Intl. Workshop organized by Solidarity Centre, Washington at Bangkok. Thailand from Oct. 8-11.

Ramachandhar. P. (1964) : *Attitudes of women to part-time employment*. Part-1 Report. Department of Social Research. Tata Institute of Social Science. Bombay.

Raman. R. Anant (1989) : "A Review of Free Trade Zones in Developing Countries" *Indian Institute of Foreign Trade*. New Delhi.

Rao. D.V. (1992) : *Status of Women and Children in Slums: A study of Hyderabad City*, Navrang, New Delhi.

Reddy. P.R. (1998) : *Women in Development*, Vol. 1&2. B.R.Publishing Corporation, Delhi.

Sharma & Sengupta (1984) : "Women Employment at SEEPZ. Unit for Urban Studies. T.I.S.S. Bumbay. (Report prepared for Insian Council for Research on International Economic Relations, New Delhi).

Sharmila Peieis & Ranaraja. S. (2001) : *Labour Issues in Export Processing Zones in South Asia*, I.L.O., New Delhi.

Singh etal, Andrea Menifee Singh and Souze, A.D. (1976) : *The Urban Poor*, Manohar publication, New Delhi.

Singh, A and Souze, A.D. (1976) : *Position of women in important basis in Delhi*, ISI Mimeo.

Singh, A.M. (1978) : "Rural Urban Migration of Women among the Urban Poor in India: Causes and Consequences, *Social Action*, 28 (4).

Sinha, J.N. (1961) : *Indian working force*–Its growth changing Composition. Censes of India.

Skeldon, Ronald (1997) : "Rural-urban Migration and Its Implications for Poverty Alleviation", *Asia-Pacific Population Journal*, 12 (1).

Standing, G. and Skedeo, F. : "Labour Migration and Development in Gayana" in *International Labour Review*, Nov.- Dec., Vol. 116, No. 3.

Statutory Commission. (2003) : "Women's Employment in a Changing World" *Women and Economy-2003*.

Sudha Despande (1993) : "Structural Adjustment and Feminisation", in Alkh N. Sharma, Seema Singh (Ed) *Women and Work-Changing scenario in India, Indian Society of Labour Economics*, Patna, B.P Publishing Corporation, New Delhi.

Sukle Bose (1985) : "Caste, Trade and female labour participation", *Social Change*, Vol. 15. No. 2.june.

Sulbha Brehme (1979) : *Economic plight of Tamil women in Pune*, ICSSR, Mimeo.

Sundari, S. (2005) : "Migration as a Livelihood Strategy A Gender Perspective" *Economic and Political Weekly*, May 28 – June 4.

Sunder (1981) : "Characteristics of Female Employment, Implications of Research and Policy", *Economic and Political Weekly*, Bombay, 9th May.

Sunder Pushpa (1981) : "Characteristic of female employment-implication of Research and Policy", *Economic and Political Weekly*, Vol XVI No.19. May.

Surinder Jetley (1990) : "Women in the Food Processing Industry" in Divya Pandey & Mira Savara (ed), 'Between the Farm and Thali-Women and Food Processing, Research Centre for Women Studies. S.N.D.T. Women's University, Bombay.

Sushma Singhal (1995) : *Development of Education Occupation and Employment of Women in India*, Mittal Publication, Delhi.

Thamargoshi, R. (2001) : *Promotion of social dialogue in EPZs in South Asia*, Synthesis of Experience. Ed. by A.S. Oberoi & Others.

Theador Caplow (1954) : *The sociology of work*, the University of Minnesota Press, Minneopolis.

Thomas, D.S. (1993) : "Research Memorandum on Migration Differentials", *Social Science Research Council Bulletin*, 43, New York.

Tirupati Town (1987) : PhD thesis, Australian National University, Canberra.

UNDP (1991) : *Human Development Report*, Oxford University Press, New York.

UNIDO (1995) : *Export Processing Zones: Principles and Practices*, Vienna, UNIDO.

Usha Kundra (1999) : "Employment opportunities for women in changing Society", *Kurukshetra*, Department of Humanities, Regional Engineering College.

Veena; Shatrugna (1994) : "Women and Health", *The Indian Journal of Social Science*, Vol. 7, Nos. 3 &4, Sage Publication, New Delhi.

Venkata Ratnam, C.S. (2001) : *Labour Issues in Export Processing Zones in South Asia: Role of Social Dialogue*, South Asia Multidisciplinary Team (SAAT), New Delhi.

Vijay; Rukmini Rao & Subha Hussain (1991) : " Invisible Hand- The Women Behind India's Export Earnings" in Nirmala Banerjee (ed) *Indian Women in changing Industrial Scenario*, Sage Publications, New Delhi.

Visaria, P. (1976) : "Employment – A Trend Report: A Survey of Research in Economics", Vol.No.11, *Macro Economics*, Chapter III.

W.H.O. (1972) : *Health Hazards of Human Environment*, Geneva.

W.H.O. (1973) : *Environmental and Health Monitoring in Occupational Health*, Geneva.

W.H.O. (Technical Report Series No. 66) (1953) : *Joint ILO/WHO Committee on Occupational Health* (Second Report), Geneva.

Whyte, R.O. (1982) : *The Rural Women of Asia*, Colorado.

Wood, C. (1981) : Structural Change and Household Strategies: A Conceptual Framework for the Study of Rural Migration, *Human Organisation,* 40 (4).

World H *in*

Organisa

Yadav, Y

CPSIA information can be obtained
at www.ICGtesting.com
Printed in the USA
BVHW060850140123
656278BV00010B/1166

9 781805 454151